Upper Intermediate

Just

For class or
self-study

Listening and Speaking

Jeremy Harmer
& Carol Lethaby

mc Marshall Cavendish
Education

D1440588

Photo acknowledgements

p.8 ©Bill Varie/Corbis; p.12 a ©Luca I. Tettoni/Corbis, b ©Jeremy Harmer, c ©Jeremy Harmer, d ©Hulton-Deutsch Collection/CORBIS; p.15 top ©Hag, 1 ©Hag/Special Photographers Library, 2 ©Hag/Special Photographers Library; p.16 left ©Ingram Publishing/Alamy, right ©Royalty Free/Corbis; p.18 a ©Alan MacWeeney/Corbis, b ©Buzz Pictures/Alamy, c ©Scott Hortop/Alamy, d ©Royalty Free/Corbis, e ©Brand X Pictures/Alamy, Marcus ©Royalty Free/Corbis, Danny ©Royalty Free/Corbis, Carmen ©Ron Chapple/Thinkstock/Alamy, Ellie ©Bob Thomas/Alamy, Jack ©Royalty Free/Corbis; p.20 top far left ©Royalty Free/Corbis, left ©Jim McGuire/Index Stock/Alamy, centre ©Royalty Free/Corbis, right ©gkphotography/Alamy, far right ©Kelly Redinger/Design Pics Inc/Alamy, bottom far left ©Aflo Foto Agency/Alamy, left ©ICIMAGE/Alamy, centre ©Tom Wagner/Corbis Saba, right ©Yavuz Arslan/Black Star/Alamy, far right ©Scott Hortop/Alamy; p.30 a ©Shout/Alamy, b ©Owen Franken/Corbis, c ©Owen Franken/Corbis, d ©Steve McDonough/Corbis, e ©Royalty Free/Corbis, bottom far left ©Image 100/Alamy, left ©ImageState/Royalty Free/Alamy, centre ©Image100/Alamy, right ©Cameron/Corbis, far right ©Royalty Free/Corbis; p.32 ©Island Records, used with kind permission of Nick Drake's estate; p.34 ©Jean Pierre Amet/Corbis; p.37 left ©Corbis Sygma, centre ©Corbis Sygma, right ©Rex Features; p.39 Peter MacDiarmid/Rex Features; p.44 ©Jan Blake used with kind permission; p.47 both ©Van Gogh Museum used with kind permission; p.54 right ©Buzz Pictures/Alamy, left ©Royalty Free Corbis; p.56 top ©Scott Hortop/Alamy, bottom ©Oliver Furrer/Brand X Pictures; p.72 ©Corbis Sygma

Text acknowledgements

p.33 Northern Sky (Nick Drake) used by permission of Warlock Music Ltd. Available on the Nick Drake compilation A Treasury; p.37 Gladiator based upon original storyline from www.dreamworksfansite.com/gladiator/storyline/storyline.htm; p.40 White Teeth by Zadie Smith, published by Hamish Hamilton, 2000, ©Zadie Smith 2000; p.50 Small Boy by Norman MacCraig, ©Birlinn; p.53 Little House on the Prairie by Laura Ingalls Wilder, reproduced by kind permission of HarperCollins Children's Books (USA); p.70 Longman Dictionary of Contemporary English 4, ©Pearson Education;

Audio acknowledgements

Audio Script: p.81 Interview with Hag and Jeremy Harmer, reproduced kindly by Hag; p.81 Little House on the Prairie by Laura Ingalls Wilder, reproduced by kind permission of HarperCollins Children's Books (USA); p.81 White Teeth by Zadie Smith, published by Hamish Hamilton, 2000, ©Zadie Smith 2000; p.87-88 Interview between Jan Black & Presenter, reproduced kindly by Jan Blake; p.89 Small Boy by Norman MacCraig, ©Birlinn; Northern Sky, taken from the Nick Drake compilation A Treasury.

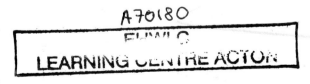
© 2005 Marshall Cavendish Ltd

First published 2005 by Marshall Cavendish Ltd

Marshall Cavendish is a member of the Times Publishing Group

Marshall Cavendish ELT
119 Wardour Street
London W1F 0UW

Designed by Hart McLeod, Cambridge
Editorial development by Ocelot Publishing, Oxford, with Geneviève Talon

Printed and bound by EDELVIVES, Spain

A70180

Contents

Skills titles available at intermediate level

Just Reading and Writing 0-462-00711-1

Just Grammar 0-462-00713-8

Just Listening and Speaking 0-462-00714-6 (with Audio CD)

Just Vocabulary 0-462-00712-X (with Audio CD)

Introduction

For the student

Just Listening and Speaking (Upper Intermediate) is one of two skills books designed for you to study on your own, or together with other students and a teacher. It will help you improve your understanding of spoken English, and you will improve your speaking too.

We have chosen the listening extracts and speaking tasks carefully to offer an interesting and challenging mix of topics and activities. With the listening extracts there are exercises to help you understand them and learn new language from them. In the speaking activities we help you do the tasks successfully, and there are exercises looking at the difference between speaking and writing.

There is an accompanying CD with all the listening extracts and speaking examples. When you see this symbol ( ) it means that you can listen to the CD. You will also find an audioscript near the back of the book.

When you see this symbol ( ) it means that the answers to the exercises are in the answer key at the back of the book. You can check your answers there.

We are confident that this book will help you become a better listener and speaker of English. Enjoy using it!

For the teacher

The *Just* skills books at the Upper Intermediate level can be used on their own or in combination, or as supplementary material to support other materials. They have been written and designed using a consistent methodological approach that allows them to be used easily together. They are designed in such a way that they can either be used in class or by the students working on their own.

Just Listening and Speaking consists of 18 listening units in Part A and four speaking sections in Part B. The listening extracts include news broadcasts, stories, dramas, comedy, authentic interviews, audiobook extracts and a beautiful song. There are comprehension and language extension exercises to accompany each listening extract. In Part B students get practice in reading aloud and interacting with speakers on the audio tracks (for interviews, dialogues, etc). Section 4 makes them aware of some of the most obvious differences between spoken and written English.

All the listening extracts and interactive spoken material for Part B are on the accompanying CD. There is an audioscript at the back of the book, together with a comprehensive answer key where students can check their work.

Our aim has been to provide texts and tasks that are themselves stimulating and that could lead to any number of student activities once the exercises in this book have been completed.

We are confident that you will find this book a real asset and that you will also want to try the other title at the Upper Intermediate level, *Just Reading and Writing*.

Part A: Listening

Money advice

1 Listen to Track 1. Circle the best answer.

Don wants to:
a ... learn how to invest money.
b ... talk about how to pay his debts.
c ... find out how to make more money.
d ... manage his money better.

I have a commitment to providing independent financial advice for people who are looking to invest money, buy a house, talk about how to pay off difficult debts, prepare for retirement or just simply for those who want to understand money better and make it work for them. I've been a personal financial advisor for ten years and I listen carefully to you and your financial needs and goals.

Make an appointment today – you won't regret it.

SUZANNE MOORE *Independent Financial Advice*

www.MooreAdvice.com

1-800-273-0903

2 Listen to Track 2 and complete the advisor's notes.

Suzanne Moore - Independent Financial Advice	
Spends now	**Ways to save**
Spends (**a**) $ .... per week on food.	Shop at (**b**) ....
Goes to (**c**) .... four times a week.	Go (**d**) .... a week.
Spends (**e**) .... on rent.	Maybe find somewhere cheaper.
Buys (**f**) .... a week.	Only buy one.
Goes to the movies once a week.	Go (**g**) ....
Eats in the (**h**)	Make a sandwich at home.

3 **Listen to Tracks 1 and 2 again. Complete these sentences with the words you hear.**

a I'm not a big .... , but I just can't seem to make ends meet.

b I'm an English Lit. .... , so I have a lot of work.

c Hmm. That's a .... , isn't it?

d You're going to have to make a ....

e ... whatever you spend your money on – your ....

f And then on the other side, you write down what you could change and
.... on to save money.

g How much money do you spend on .... per week?

h It .... from one week to the next, but I'd guess about $100.

i They often have good prices and ....

j ... and try to share the expenses with your ....

4 **What do these words and expressions you found to complete the sentences in Activity 3 mean? Write your answers below.**

a ....

b ....

c ....

d ....

e ....

f ....

g ....

h ....

i ....

j ....

5 **How would you qualify Suzanne Moore's advice? Choose two out of these five words.**

prudent

original

rash

down-to-earth

careless

Telling a joke

1 Look at the picture and choose the best interpretation for it.

a The man is a doctor and he's trying to help the woman.
b The woman is trying to ignore someone who is talking too much.
c The man is trying to persuade the woman to marry him.
d The woman is so bored that she has fallen asleep.
e Something else.

Listen to Track 3 and check your answer.

2 Listen to Track 4 and circle the correct answer.

a The man pays the woman   £5   £10   £20
b The woman pays the man   £2   £5   £20

3 Listen to Track 4 again and check whether these statements are true or false according to what you hear.

	True	False
a The man wants to sleep.		
b The woman is not interested in the game.		
c The man tells her the rules of the game.		
d The man makes the game more tempting for her so that she will play.		
e The woman thinks that if she plays the game, the man will leave her alone.		
f She does not know the answer to the question he asks.		
g The question she asks is more difficult than the man expected.		
h The man tries to find the answer in more than one place.		
i The woman knows the answer to the question she asks.		

4 Complete the sentences below with words and expressions from Tracks 3 and 4.

a He just won't ....

b The guy keeps asking her questions and then, to .... , he turns to her and …

c … and closes her eyes to go to sleep, hoping that he'll ....

d Even though she .... , he tells her the rules.

e The woman analyses the situation and .... that the only way to get some sleep is to …

f The man is .... when he asks the first question.

g He thought this was going to be .... for him.

h 'I don't know the answer!' he whispers, ... with despair.

i The man is completely ....

j 'Please .... ,' he pleads.

5 Write the letter of the words or expressions from Activity 4 which can be replaced by the words or expressions below.

1 understand   ....

2 very enthusiastic   ....

3 realises   ....

4 make me feel better ....

5 very surprised   ....

6 stop talking   ....

7 is not at all interested ....

8 crying   ....

9 very easy   ....

10 add to the problem ....

6 What do you think makes the joke funny?

a It is a misunderstanding about language.
b The woman makes a fool out of the man.
c It is the unusual and clever way she fools the man.
d It is the way the joke teller tells the story.

What photographs remind us of

1 Listen to Track 5. Match the photographs with the speakers. The speakers are in the right order.

Peter ....

Jane ....

Kate ....

Betty ....

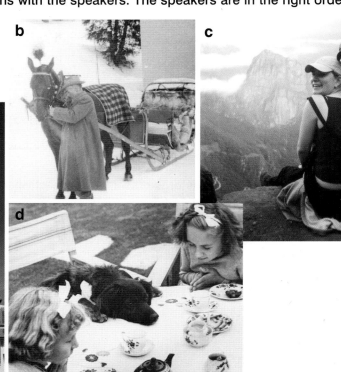

How old do you think the speakers are? Why?

Peter... Kate...

Jane... Betty...

2 Who:

a ... learnt to ski when he was young?

b ... once had a box camera?

c ... has a mother who teaches?

d ... has lived in various different countries?

e ... visited Bolivia?

f ... went to a place that looked better than pictures of it do?

g ... didn't enjoy school in Johannesburg very much?

h ... used to go for long walks?

i ... had a seaside holiday every summer?

j ... had a sister who went to Chile?

k ... acted like a tourist guide?

3 Listen to Track 5 again. What are the speakers talking about? Write one of the names in the blanks (you will use some names more than once).

Arosa
Bangkok
Cuzco
Machu Picchu
Sally
Thailand
The Grand Palace

a I loved it better than some of the other places. ....

b It dates back to the 18th century. ....

c It was really cool. ....

d It was really great. ....

e It's a fabulous old Inca city. ....

f It's a fantastic place. ....

g It's much much better than any photograph you see of it. ....

h It's the old capital of the Inca empire. ....

i They'd decided to learn how to ski. ....

j We went everywhere together. ....

k You leave it to walk the Inca trail. ....

4 Listen to Track 5 again or look at the audioscript. Match the words and phrases in italics in the first column with their equivalent meanings in the second column.

a *diplomat*

b *fabulous*

c *I'd so like* to go back

d *it dates back to* the 18th century

e *it's not a patch on the real thing*

f *kind of like* tourist guides

g *primitive*

h *scenery*

i *slopes*

j Thailand was *really cool*

k the dog *passed away*

l *trail*

1 a path, usually in the wilderness

2 as if we were

3 died

4 enjoyable

5 I would very much like

6 it happened / was built in

7 it is not as good or impressive as the thing itself

8 really fantastic

9 sides of mountains that people ski down

10 someone who works for their government, but in an embassy in a different country

11 the countryside (mountains, rivers, etc.) that you see before you

12 very old-fashioned, unsophisticated

a	e	i ....
b	f	j ....
c	g	k ....
d	h	l ....

Combination pictures

1 Listen to Track 6 and circle the best answer.

 a 'Hag' is short for Ian.
 b Most people call Ian James Hargreaves 'Hag'.
 c Everyone calls Ian James Hargreaves 'Hag'.
 d 'Hag' was the name Ian James Hargreaves chose
 for himself when he was six or seven.

2 Look at the pictures (*1* and *2*) and listen to Track 7. Write *1*, *2*,
or both *1* and *2* next to the statements on the next page.

a Hag doesn't really like it.   ....

b It earned Hag a lot of money.   ....

c It is 'exactly what it says it is'.   ....

d It is a combination picture.   ....

e It is made by exposing the same piece of photographic
   paper to a number of different enlargers.   ....

f It is made out of more than one original photograph.   ....

g Many people have bought it.   ....

h People like it.   ....

i You can find it on pillowcases.   ....

j You have to be patient to make it.   ....

k You make it by printing bits of different negatives onto
   the same piece of paper.   ....

3 Match the words and phrases with their definitions.

a a storm in a teacup	1 image on film that shows dark areas as light and vice versa
b abstract	2 another word for picture
c blended	3 bits
d duvet	4 showing shapes and colours, but not real objects
e elements	5 mixed together
f enlargers	6 photographic machines to make an image bigger
g flattering	7 pleasing because people have a high opinion of you or your work
h image	8 something like a blanket to cover you in bed
i negative	9 a completely exaggerated situation (like an unnecessary row)

a .... b .... c .... d .... e .... f .... g .... h .... i ....

4 Listen to Track 8. Is the following statement true or false?

Hag believes that computers and digital technology have made film obsolete.

5 Listen to Track 8 again and complete the following extracts with one word for each blank.

• I have to have a (**a**) .... Doesn't matter whether I use it or not but it has to be there.
  I don't feel (**b**) .... without it.

• And there we are sitting around a table eating meals with (**c**) .... because it's nice, because
  they have a certain quality that you cannot get anywhere else except by a (**d**) ....
  (**e**) .... and that live (**f**) .... on the table has a certain essence that you do
  not get from a (**g**) ....

• Now people will pay for that rather than buy a (**h**) .... file that's been created on a
  (**i**) .... and then (**j**) .... , no matter how well. It's not the same thing, it's a
  (**k**) .... of a (**l**) .... file.

A story about wolves

1 **Listen to Track 9 and say which of these three books the extract comes from.**

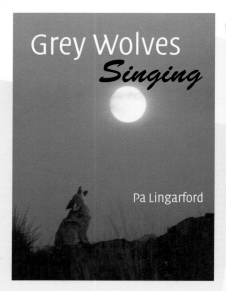

A study of wolf behaviour in the wild, discussing how man has tried hard to eradicate them. Written by a British author, published in 2002.

An American story for children about a family who build their own log cabin in the wild before the days of cars, telephones and electricity. Published in 1935.

The autobiography of the American Sasha Kleinstock, telling how a girl from a poor family ended up one of the richest women in the world. Published in 1997.

2 **Listen to Track 10 and then answer these questions.**

a What woke the girl up?

....

b What did she see?

....

c What did she hear?

....

d Who protected her?

....

e What stopped the girl being frightened?

....

3 Answer the questions *a–d*.

a What is a quilt and how many are mentioned in the extract?

....

b Who or what is Jack?

....

c Why does the writer talk about window-holes instead of windows?

....

d Who is Mary?

....

4 Listen again to Track 10 and complete the following extracts from the story with between one and five words.

a Jack .... his teeth.

b She wanted to go to Pa, but ....
bother him now.

c He stood his gun against the wall and ....
to the window-hole.

d Laura lifted her toes into a crack in the wall and she ....
on the window slab, and she looked and looked at that wolf.

e When they saw Pa and Laura looking out, the middle of the circle
.... way.

f Go to sleep. Jack and I will ....

g She lay and listened to the breathing of the wolves ....
the log wall.

Things people do for fun

1 Look at the pastimes *a–e* and then look at the five people.
  Which people do which pastimes, do you think?

a fishing / angling

b potholing

c train-spotting

d golf

e skydiving

a .... b .... c .... d .... e ....

Marcus   Danny   Carmen   Ellie   Jack

Listen to Track 11. Were you correct?

2 Listen again. Who says … ?

a It gives you time to think.   ....
b I've begged her to stop.   ....
c And that's the truth.   ....
d I've never had any trouble.   ....
e I'll take your word for it.   ....
f The only downside is that it can be pretty cold. ....
g I'm not addicted to it or anything.   ....
h You can't be serious.   ....
i It's not for everybody.   ....
j People call us nerds in anoraks.   ....

3 Look at the meanings and match them with the sentences in Activity 2 in which they appear. Write a–j in the spaces provided.

1 I've asked as strongly as possible.   ....
2 I could easily stop doing it.   ....
3 I believe you, but I don't want to try it. ....
4 Only some people enjoy it.   ....
5 very boring people who are interested in silly
   little details (slang)   ....
6 the one disadvantage   ....
7 That's a ridiculous suggestion.   ....

4 Sentences from Track 11 have got mixed up. Can you re-write them, by crossing out the incorrect part and finding the correct second half in each case? The first one is done for you.

a I call it crawling through underground caves. ~~It's just wonderful.~~
   I call it crawling through underground caves on your hands and knees.

b It's just that feeling of surfing the sky, like my Dad.
   ....

c Oh dear. But we aren't doing anybody any harm.
   ....

d Oh no, I'm not addicted to it or anything. It gives you time to think.
   ....

e People call us nerds in anoraks, I know, I suppose that means I am a bit of an addict, doesn't it!
   ....

f Sometimes, a little, but you get that rush of adrenaline, on your hands and knees.
   ....

g That's why I like it. It's something I do just for fun.
   ....

h The only downside is that it can be pretty cold and I've never had any trouble.
   ....

i Well yes, but I've been potholing for ten years now just standing on a station platform all day.
   ....

j Yeah. I'm an angler, plunging through the air.
   ....

Leisure centre

1 Look at these pictures of leisure centre activities and tick the ones that you would expect to see at a leisure centre in the blue box.

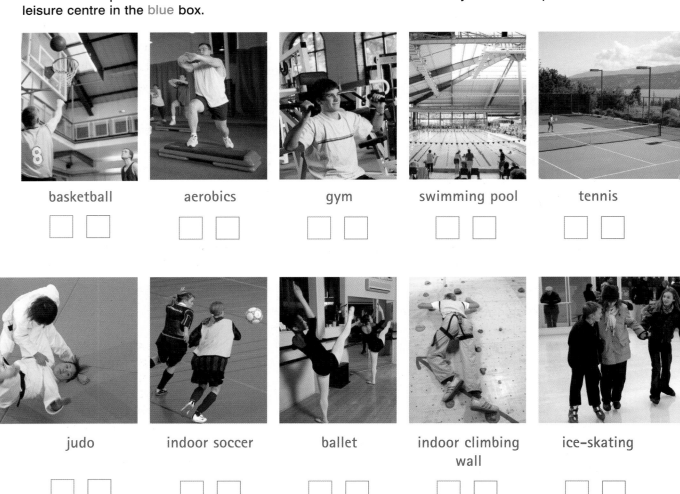

basketball ☐ ☐

aerobics ☐ ☐

gym ☐ ☐

swimming pool ☐ ☐

tennis ☐ ☐

judo ☐ ☐

indoor soccer ☐ ☐

ballet ☐ ☐

indoor climbing wall ☐ ☐

ice-skating ☐ ☐

Now listen to Track 12 and tick which activities are mentioned in the red box.

2 Listen to Track 12 again and choose the correct answer according to what you hear.

a To become a member of High Park Leisure Centre, you should:
   1 ... hang up and call the correct extension.
   2 ... push the number 2 button on the phone.
   3 ... stay on the line and wait for someone.

b The High Park Leisure Centre is open:
   1 ... every day of the week.
   2 ... on New Year's Day.
   3 ... at the same times every day.

c If you are under 13:
   1 ... you must pay £10 to skate.
   2 ... you may not skate alone.
   3 ... you cannot rent skates.

d If you pay £5 for the day, you can:
   1 ... use the swimming pool and the gym.
   2 ... only use the swimming pool.
   3 ... use the gym, but not the pool.

e You can play tennis any time:
   1 ... when the Leisure Centre team has a match.
   2 ... by dialing extension 67 of the Centre.
   3 ... there is a free court available.

f A ballet class lasts:
   1 ... until January 15th.
   2 ... for a whole year.
   3 ... for ten weeks.

g If you go online, you can:
   1 ... register for a class over the phone.
   2 ... get a special discount.
   3 ... see what classes are available.

h By pressing 1, you will:
   1 ... speak to a representative.
   2 ... hear the information again.
   3 ... end the phone call.

3 Match the first half of sentences (a–l) from Track 12 with their second halves (1–11). Careful: there is one first half too many.

a Our classes
b If you know the extension of the person you are calling,
c If you would like information about our facilities and opening hours,
d If you would like to become a member of the Centre,
e If you would like to speak to a Leisure Centre representative,
f All children under 13 must be accompanied by an adult
g Please call 01 800 6767 extension 54
h Please take advantage of our online booking service
i Thank you
j If you would like to hear this information again,
k The High Park swimming pool is open all year round and
l We are open every day of the year

1 ... for calling the High Park Leisure Centre.
2 ... please press 3.
3 ... please press 1.
4 ... at www.highparkleisurecentre.co.uk
5 ... last for ten weeks.
6 ... for details of availability and prices.
7 ... costs £3.50 or £1 for members of the High Park Leisure Centre.
8 ... except 25th December and New Year's Day.
9 ... please stay on the line.
10 ... please press 2.
11 ... please put in that number now.

a ....   b ....   c ....   d ....   e ....   f ....
g ....   h ....   i ....   j ....   k ....   l ....

4 Match these words from Track 12 with a synonym or definition (*1–8*).

a leisure   1 rooms, equipment, etc. that you can use

b facilities   2 competitions, games

c take advantage of   3 with

d concludes   4 places to play tennis, badminton or squash

e accompanied by   5 look at

f courts   6 free time

g matches   7 ends, finishes

h consult   8 use

a .... b .... c .... d .... e .... f .... g .... h ....

5 Now use one of the words or expressions (*a–h*) from Activity 4 in the sentences below.

a I'm going to .... the dictionary to find the meaning of this word.

b We need to .... of this good weather and finish painting the outside of the house, before it starts to rain.

c This piece .... our concert for tonight. We hope you enjoyed it and look forward to seeing you again.

d The players came out onto the .... and the crowd started to cheer. They took out their racquets and began to warm up.

e The famous actor was seen at the party .... an unknown woman and their photo was on the front page of the tabloid newspapers the next day.

f She doesn't know what to do with her life – I think she has too much .... time on her hands and she needs to get a job.

g The new school has state-of-the-art .... , including a new science lab and a huge computer room.

h I just play tennis for fun now, I don't take part in .... any more.

The radio lecture

1 Here are some of the words you will hear in the lecture. What do they mean? What is the talk going to be about, do you think? Write your prediction in the space provided.

bell
experiment
fur coat
press a bar
rabbit
rat
ring
salivate
theory

....

....

....

Listen to Track 13. Were you correct?

2 Listen to Track 13 again and put the following summary sentences in the appropriate order.

a A modern view of Watson and Raynor's experiment is that it wasn't very ethical. [ ]

b An example of behaviourist research is the work of Watson and Raynor. [ ]

c Conditioning is not the only way of learning. [ ]

d Behaviourism involves habit formation. [ ]

e Experiments with dogs and rats have shown behaviourism at work. [ ]

f The theory of behaviourism has had a big impact on learning. [ ]

g There are different theories of learning. [ ]

h Watson and Raynor wanted to reverse their experiment. [ ]

3 Listen to Track 13 again, and put the following in the correct place in the table. Some words can go in more than one column.

bar	frightened	noise
bell	fur coat	phobia
dogs	habit formation	prize
1900–1950	influential	rabbit
food	light	Russia

Albert	Behaviourism	Pavlov	Rats

Add further notes if you wish.

. . . .

4 Answer the questions.

a What do you understand by 'habit formation'?

....

b What did Pavlov's dogs think when they heard the bell?

....

c What did the rats learn to do in the end?

....

d Who was Albert?

....

e Why did Albert become frightened of his pet rabbit?

....

f What was the effect of other animals and fur on Albert?

....

g What was the response of Albert's parents to the researchers' desire to reverse the experiment?

....

5 How good is your memory? Complete the following extract from the lecture with one word for each blank.

The theory of behaviourism is (a) .... : if you make someone do something and

(b) .... them a prize, a reward when they do it (c) .... , and if you do this again and

again and again, (d) .... they will learn to do it every time, and (e) .... they have

learnt to do it in this (f) .... it will, in the end, no longer be (g) .... to give them

that prize. The whole (h) .... of behaviourism, in other words, (i) .... on habit

formation – that is getting people so (j) .... to a task that they do it without (k) ....

There are many examples of this (l) .... of habit formation. The Russian researcher Pavlov,

for (m) .... , taught his dogs that the sound of a bell ringing (n) .... that they were

going to be given food. As a (o) .... , every time he rang the bell the dogs salivated –

(p) .... , in the end, when there was no (q) .... Then there were all the

experiments with (r) .... When the rats saw a light, they (s) .... to press a bar in their

cages. (t) .... they pressed the bar they got some (u) .... They did it again and

again and again. In the (v) .... they learnt to press the bar *every time* they saw the

(w) ....

The paranormal

1 The words on the right are all examples of 'paranormal' beliefs. Which ones are connected with talking about the future? Write *F* on the line.

a astrology	.....	f magic	.....
b ESP	.....	g palmistry	.....
c faith–healing	.....	h tarot cards	.....
d fortune-telling	.....	i telepathy	.....
e ghosts	.....	j UFOs	.....

2 Now listen to Track 14. Who is the 'believer'? Who is the 'sceptic'?

a The man is the ....

b The woman is the ....

3 Listen to Track 14 again and match the beginnings of the sentences in the first column (*a–g*) with the ends of the sentences in the second column (*1–7*).

a The man thinks that
b Dr Hyman became a sceptic when
c The man believes that if
d The woman thinks that the man
e When the woman calls the man 'Mr Clever', she is
f The woman thinks that
g The man likes

1 … without mystery life is very boring.
2 … is too cynical.
3 … he deliberately read someone's palm badly and they said it was accurate.
4 … the woman.
5 … we hear things often enough, we start to believe them.
6 … there is a rational explanation for everything.
7 … making fun of him in a friendly way.

a .... b .... c .... d .... e .... f .... g ....

4 Listen to Track 14 again and complete this summary of the conversation.

Two people are eating (**a**) .... in a (**b**) .... They seem to have a friendly relationship. They start talking about the (**c**) .... and the man surprises the woman by (**d**) .... that he doesn't believe in any paranormal phenomena. His cynicism (**e**) .... when he heard an American professor talking about an (**f**) .... from his youth. Against the protests of the woman, the man suggests that he (**g**) .... write a zodiac description of her without (**h**) .... anything about astrology. He believes that there is always a (**i**) .... explanation for everything, but that people start to (**j**) .... things if they see or hear them often enough. The woman thinks that it is a pity that the man is so (**k**) .... since it makes his life less (**l**) .... The man admits that there is only one mystery he doesn't have the (**m**) .... to.

. . . .

5 What does the man say about:

a ... crystal balls?

....

b ... tea leaves?

....

c ... 'Your stars' in the newspaper?

....

d ... people who have lived 'past lives'?

....

e ... people who see flying saucers?

....

f ... people's responses to suggestion?

....

. . . .

6 Complete these utterances from Track 14 with one word for each gap.

a So you .... that stuff now?

b Oh come on, you're not saying all that is .... ?

c .... doing so far?

d There isn't any mystery ....

e How do you figure .... ?

f You wouldn't believe it, ... ?

g Well if there isn't any mystery in life, ... ?

h Well now, that ....

The driving lesson

1 **Match the words with the pictures.**

a accelerator ....

b brake ....

c clutch ....

d gear stick ....

e radiator ....

f rear-view mirror ....

g steering-wheel ....

h wing mirror ....

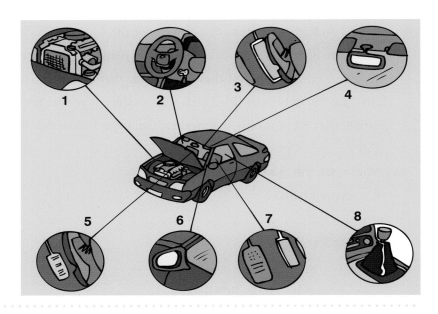

2 **Listen to Track 15. True or false?**

a Mr Radinski has not driven before. [ ]

b Mr Radinski's father is a farmer. [ ]

c Mr Radinski never had any problems driving
before this lesson. [ ]

d Mr Radinski hits a pedestrian at a roundabout. [ ]

e The pedestrian is a woman. [ ]

f Mr Radinski hits a lorry at a roundabout. [ ]

g Mr Radinski is a good driver. [ ]

3 **Listen to Track 15 again.
Complete the map showing
where the impact took place.
Use the following symbol for
the car which Mr Radinski was
driving.**

4   Complete these two extracts with the words Mr Radinski spoke (but which we don't hear on Track 15). The first one is done for you.

1

INSTRUCTOR: Well now, Mr Radinski, have you ever driven a car before?

RADINSKI: (**a**) ...Yes, I have. ....

RADINSKI: (**b**) ....

RADINSKI: (**c**) ....

RADINSKI: (**d**) ....

INSTRUCTOR: ... and your father is buying some new wing mirrors because you drove too close to the fence ...

2

INSTRUCTOR: Yes, yes, Mr Radinski ... the truck driver was very rude ...

RADINSKI: (**a**) ....

RADINSKI: (**b**) ....

RADINSKI: (**c**) ....

RADINSKI: (**d**) ....

RADINSKI: (**e**) ....

RADINSKI: (**f**) ....

INSTRUCTOR: Yes, yes, Mr Radinski. That is the end of this lesson.

---

5   Choose complements for the verbs (some can be used with more than one verb).

Verbs	Complements
a adjust	**1** neutral
b put	**2** the accelerator
c put your foot on	**3** the brake
d release	**4** the clutch
e select	**5** the engine
f switch off	**6** the engine into first gear
g switch on	**7** the handbrake
h take your foot off	**8** the mirror
i turn	**9** the steering-wheel

a ....   b ....   c ....   d ....   e ....

f ....   g ....   h ....   i ....

Which verbs are not in the recording? Which noun is not in the recording?

....

....

What people like to eat

1 Look at the pictures of the restaurants. Which person would like to eat in which restaurant, do you think? Write *a–e* next to their names in the first box. Which of these places would you like to eat at and why?

| Chris | | | Jed | | | Julia | | | Martin | | | Naomi | |

Listen to Track 16 and write the correct letter of the restaurant in the second box. How good were your predictions?

2 **Listen to Track 16 again. Who:**

a ... doesn't like eating in expensive restaurants? ....

b ... is keen on cleanliness? ....

c ... is well known in the restaurant where he goes? ....

d ... likes self-service restaurants? ....

e ... likes to know everything on the menu? ....

f ... often tries food they haven't eaten before? ....

g ... sometimes eats a little and sometimes eats a lot at the same restaurant? ....

h ... takes girlfriends to restaurants so that he can get to know them? ....

i ... thinks that the experience of eating is as important as the food? ....

j ... thinks the people who serve at the restaurant are well-mannered? ....

k ... thinks there are many factors to finding the perfect restaurant? ....

l ... wears ordinary work clothes to eat in the restaurant? ....

3 **Write the initial letter(s) (*C*, *Je*, *Ju*, *M*, *N*) of the name of the person who says these things.**

a A restaurant is a great place to take someone on a date. ....

b For me the best way to eat is – you get in, get served quickly, get out and get on with your life. ....

c I don't mind paying for good food and delightful surroundings. ....

d I go there in my work clothes – it's cheap too. ....

e I like plain food, that's not spicy, but nice and fresh. ....

f I love the whole restaurant-going experience. ....

g I love these self-service places where you can eat as much as you want. ....

h The food's not delicious, but it's good, if fills you up and it's great value. ....

i You can't beat a place with lovely home-cooked food and friendly service. ....

j You need your date's attention to be on you, not on the people around you or the music. ....

4 **Complete the table with notes on what the speakers say about these things in the type of restaurant they like.**

	Food	Service	Atmosphere	Price
Chris				
Jed				
Julia				
Martin				
Naomi				

Northern Sky

1 Read the two Internet comments about the song 'Northern Sky' from the album *Bryter Layter* by British singer-songwriter Nick Drake, and answer the questions which follow.

Arlene

It's almost impossible to pick my favorite Nick song, but if I absolutely had to choose I guess I'd go with the one that many Nick fans pick, 'Northern Sky', one of the most stunningly-beautiful songs ever written.

Jake

When all is said and done, this is as good a love song as any ever written; Drake's delicate vocals play against an effortless folk-rock arrangement to create yet another first-rate masterpiece.

Find:

a ... two words or expressions which mean the same as 'choose'. ....

....

b ... a word which means 'definitely'. ....

c ... an expression which means 'my considered opinion is that ...'. ....

d ... a word which means 'fine, pleasant, but not strong'. ....

e ... a phrase that means 'very high quality'. ....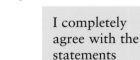

2 Listen to Track 17 ('Northern Sky'). What is your first reaction? Choose a number between 0 and 5 from the line below.

| I completely agree with the statements in Activity 1. | 5 .... 4 .... 3 .... 2 .... 1 .... 0 | I completely disagree with the statements in Activity 1. |

3 Read the lines *a–i* from the song. Listen to Track 17 again. Put the pairs of lines in the right order in the table (some lines occur more than once).

Northern Sky

a But now you're here
  Brighten my northern sky.

b I never held emotion in the palm of my hand
  Or felt sweet breezes in the top of a tree.

c Would you love me for my money?
  Would you love me for my head?

d I've been a long time that I've wandered
  Through the people I have known.

e I never felt magic crazy as this;
  I never saw moons knew the meaning of the sea.

f Oh, if you would and you could
  Come blow your horn on high.

g Oh, if you would and you could
  Straighten my new mind's eye.

h I've been a long time that I'm waiting.
  Been a long time that I'm blown.

i Would you love me through the winter?
  Would you love me 'til I'm dead?

1 ....

2 ....

3 ....

4 ....

5 ....

6 ....

7 ....

8 ....

9 ....

10 ....

11 ....

12 ....

4 In the song, find:

a ... three words that rhyme with *sky* (don't include *I*).

....

b ... four words that have the same vowel sound as *tree*.

....

c ... a word that rhymes with *blown*.

....

d ... a word that rhymes with *head*.

....

e ... a word with the same vowel sound as *crazy*.

....

Diana's story

1 Look at the picture of Diana. Guess as much as you can about who she is, where she's from, what she does, etc.

2 Listen to Track 18 and answer the following questions about Diana.

a Where is Diana from?

....

b What happened when she was 13?

....

c How did she try to get accommodation when she went to Mumbai (then called Bombay)?

....

d What time was it on Diana's watch when she knocked on the lady's door?

....

e Why do you think the lady said 'Come inside'?

....

f What lesson does Diana draw from this experience in her life?

....

3 Listen to Track 19. What did Diana win?

....

4 Use the table to make notes as you listen to Track 19 again.

What Diana was afraid of and why	a
The number of people watching the second competition	b
How she felt when she won her second big competition	c
What she did with the thing she won	d
What happened immediately after she won	e

5 Answer the questions about the words and phrases in blue. They are words and phrases that Diana uses in Tracks 18 and 19.

a What is a bedsit?

....

b What does it mean if we say that our hair is standing on end? Does Diana use exactly the same expression?

....

c If you give something your all, do you make a lot of effort or a little?

....

d When your mind goes blank, is it easy to decide what to say?

....

e If you feel euphoria, are you fantastically happy or terribly sad?

....

f If to trip means to fall over because something got in the way of your foot, what does trip over your words mean?

....

g Is a regular person an important person (like a movie star), or are they ordinary, like everyone else?

....

h What does a chaperone do?

....

i What is a cockpit and who usually sits there?

....

6 How good is your memory? Without looking back at Activities 1–5,
complete the following extracts with one word for each blank.

- Oooh you feel (**a**) .... The … you know it's, it's a saturation point. It's (**b**) .... much

  for you to digest that your (**c**) .... is stuck on your face. It was (**d**) .... on my face for

  weeks. I would (**e**) .... that crown in such a way that as (**f**) .... as I opened my eyes I

  would (**g**) .... my crown. I did that for (**h**) .... It was such a great feeling. You just

  you're just (**i**) .... and you are just numb. If that's what (**j**) .... is, you know, you you

  can't speak very (**k**) ....

- … and immediately there was a press (**l**) .... on stage itself and it's (**m**) .... ooh ooh

  ooh because you go from (**n**) .... nobody, a regular person. That's not (**o**) .... It's not

  a nobody. You go from being a regular person to being in every (**p**) .... around the world and

  everyone (**q**) ....

Listen to Track 19 again to check your answers.

Gladiator

1 Read the following text carefully. Can you identify the people in each photograph?

Gladiator, starring the actor Russell Crowe, was one of the first great movie hits of the 21st century. It tells the story of a heroic Roman general, Maximus Decimus Meridius, who is captured by the evil emperor Commodus. He is forced to work as a gladiator, fighting for his life for the entertainment of the crowds. Commodus hates Maximus, because Commodus' father, Marcus the old emperor, loved Maximus more than his own son.

a .... b .... c ....

2 The scene on Track 20 takes place early in the movie, and it partly explains why Commodus hates the gladiator. Marcus, the old emperor, sends for his son Commodus to see him.

Listen to Track 20 and answer the questions.

a What does Marcus tell Commodus about the future?

....

b Who is going to take over from Marcus when he dies, at least for a time?

....

c What does Marcus want to happen to Rome in the future? What does that mean?

....

d What does Commodus say that Marcus didn't want?

....

e What would have been like the 'sun on my heart for a thousand years' for Commodus?

....

f Who has failed, according to Marcus?

....

g What is the one thing that Commodus says he wants?

....

h What do you think happens at the end of the scene?

....

3 **Match the words (most of which come from Track 20) and the definitions.**

a ambition	**1** desire to succeed
b butcher	**2** bravery when in danger
c courage	**3** courage shown when you are in difficult situations
d devotion	**4** fairness in the way people are treated
e fortitude	**5** intelligence gained through experience
f justice	**6** ability to find ways of dealing with practical problems
g resourcefulness	**7** love and loyalty that you show to someone
h smother	**8** not drinking alcohol because of moral or religious beliefs
i temperance	**9** a verb which means to kill someone by putting something over their face to stop them breathing
j wisdom	**10** a verb which means to kill someone, or a lot of people, in a cruel and violent way

a .... **b** .... **c** .... **d** .... **e** ....

f .... **g** .... **h** .... **i** .... **j** ....

4 **Listen to Track 20 again. Which of the qualities were on Marcus' list?**
Which are the qualities that Commodus says he has?

5 **Read the following acting 'directions' from the original film script.**

a He kneels in front of his son. [ ]

b He stretches his arms out to Commodus, seeking forgiveness.
Commodus slowly embraces him, together they weep. [ ]

c Holding his fingers to his lips [ ]

d In anguish and tears from the disappointment of Marcus' decision [ ]

e Marcus moves his hand to touch Commodus' face and Commodus pulls away. [ ]

f Marcus still kneeling, Commodus presses his father tightly against his body,
smothering him, as Marcus struggles to be free, but fails. All the while,
Commodus cries and moans in pain, as though a child. [ ]

g Surprised at Commodus' reaction, Marcus sits. [ ]

h The smile quickly vanishes, leaving in its place painful bewilderment. [ ]

i With a slight smile on his face [ ]

Listen to Track 20 again as you read the audioscript. Match the
directions with the numbers on the script where you think they occur.

Check your guesses with the answer key at the back of the book.

White Teeth

1 Read this plot description from the book *White Teeth* by Zadie Smith and answer the questions *a–h*.

Archie (Archibald) Jones, a British man, and Samad Iqbal, originally from Bangladesh, have been friends since they were soldiers together in the British Army in World War II. They both live and work in London where Archie is married to a Jamaican woman named Clara with whom he has one nine-year-old daughter, Irie, while Samad is married to Alsana and has twin boys, Millat and Magid, who are also nine. Samad, who works as a waiter, has decided that Britain in 1984 is an unhealthy place to bring up his sons and is planning to send Magid to his family in Bangladesh in order to offer him a better education and upbringing. He has not told anyone except Archie about his plan; Magid does not know that his father is going to send him away. Archie has agreed to drive Samad and the child to the airport so that Magid can be put on the plane at 3 am.

Who:

a ... served in the British Army? ....

b ... is married to Archie? ....

c ... is Irie? ....

d ... is Samad married to? ....

e ... are Millat and Magid? ....

f ... has family in Bangladesh? ....

g ... is going to go and live in Bangladesh? ....

h ... is going to drive to the airport? ....

2 Read the following scenes from a film treatment of *White Teeth*. What, in your opinion, is the relationship between:

... Millat and Magid? ....

... Archie and Samad? ....

SCENE 25

Outside an Indian restaurant, Archie Jones is dressed in a long coat and is standing in front of his car. Samad Iqbal leaves the restaurant and approaches Archie, with his hand out to shake Archie's hand.

SAMAD	I won't forget this, Archibald.
ARCHIE	That's what friends are for, Sam, but I have to tell you something. I had to bring Millat and Irie too.
SAMAD	Why did you bring them?
ARCHIE	They all woke up when I went to get Magid.

SCENE 26

Interior of Archie's car. The three children are in the back seat, asleep, and wake up as the adults get in.

MILLAT	Hey Daddy! Where are we going, Daddy? To a secret disco party?
MAGID	Are we really? Where are we going?
IRIE	I want to go home. (*starts to cry*)

SCENE 27

Close-up on Samad's face. There are tears coming down his face. He looks straight ahead as he speaks.

SAMAD	We're going on a trip to an airport. To Heathrow.
IRIE, MILLAT, MAGID	Wow! Really?
SAMAD	And then Magid is going on a trip with Auntie Zinat.

SCENE 28

We see the three children in the back seat again.

MILLAT	Will he come back?
MAGID	Is it far? Will I be back in time for school on Monday? Only I've got to see what happens with my science experiment in photosynthesis – I put one plant in the cupboard and one plant in the sunlight and I have to see what happened.
MILLAT	Shut up about your stupid plants!
MAGID	Will I be back for school, Daddy?

SCENE 29

Close-up of Samad's face again as he struggles to answer his son.

SAMAD	You'll be in a school on Monday, Magid, I promise.

3 Listen to the same incident from the original book on Track 21. On page 40, circle:

a ... one scene that has been completely changed by the scriptwriter.
b ... some dialogue that has been changed by the scriptwriter.
c ... some dialogue that has been added by the scriptwriter.
d ... some dialogue that has been omitted by the scriptwriter.

4 Listen to Track 21 again. Are the following statements *True* or *False*? Write *T* or *F* in the brackets.

a The three children are warm.   [ ]
b The twins are excited to see their father.   [ ]
c Samad hugs his son tightly.   [ ]
d Millat doesn't want Magid to come back.   [ ]
e Samad wants to remember this car ride.   [ ]
f Archie is worried that they will not get to the airport on time. [ ]
g Magid will be able to see his science experiment on Monday.   [ ]

5 How good is your memory? Without looking back at Activities 1–4, complete
the following extracts from the book with one word for each blank.

• Samad (a) .... , clasps Archie's right hand in his own and feels the (b) ....
of his friend's fingers, feels the great (c) .... he owes him. Involuntarily, he blows
a cloud of (d) .... breath into his face. 'I won't forget this, Archibald,' he is saying.

• But Samad is already (e) .... for the door, and Archie's (f) .... must follow
the sight of three (g) .... children in the back (h) .... like a limp punch-line.

• Irie asleep; (i) .... up with her head on the ashtray and her (j) .... resting
on the gearbox, but Millat and Magid (k) .... out for their father gleefully,
(l) .... at his flares, chucking him on the chin.

• It is like a (m) .... Samad feels the tears before he can (n) .... them; he
reaches out to his (o) .... -son-by-two-minutes and holds him so tight to his
(p) .... that he snaps the arm of his (q) ....

• Years from now, even (r) .... after that plane leaves, this will be (s) ....
that Samad tries *not* to (t) .... That his memory makes no (u) .... to retain.
A sudden stone submerged. False teeth floating (v) .... to the bottom of the glass.

Now listen to Track 21 again to check your answers.

Crime doesn't pay!

1 Look at these pictures of true crimes that went wrong. Can you guess what happened?

a ....

b ....

c ....

d ....

e ....

Now listen to Track 22. Write the number of the news story next to the correct letter of the pictures.

2 Listen to Track 22 again and fill in the table with the information you hear.

	a What went wrong?	b What was stolen?
Story 1		
Story 2		
Story 3		
Story 4		
Story 5		

3 What do these words from the news reports mean?

a armoured car ....

b getaway ....

c escape route ....

d handpicked ....

e without a hitch ....

f convicted ....

g sentenced ....

h appeal ....

i prosecuted ....

j shoplifting ....

k attempted ....

l in the course of ....

m shifted ....

4 How good is your memory? Without looking back at Activities 1–4, join the following words or phrases in groups of three or four: each group relates to one story. The first one is started for you.

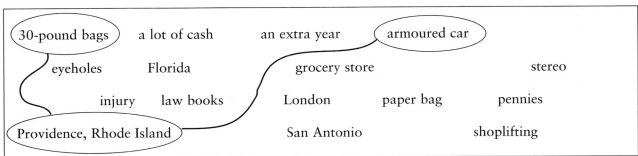

Listen to Track 22 again. Were you right?

Storyteller

1 **Using a dictionary, check the meaning of the following words and phrases.**

a   a mirror is held up   [   ]
b   asides   [   ]
c   audition   [   ]
d   being human   [   ]
e   decent money   [   ]
f   fantastic experience   [   ]
g   fascinating   [   ]
h   fundamental   [   ]
i   aren't we great?   [   ]
j   harmony   [   ]
k   hunter   [   ]
l   looked back   [   ]   r   stupid   [   ]
m   no judgement   [   ]   s   the whole gamut   [   ]
n   the place was packed   [   ]   t   visualising   [   ]
o   percussionist   [   ]   u   word for word   [   ]
p   regardless of the circumstances [   ]   v   your own subconscious   [   ]
q   something universal   [   ]   w   your own tradition   [   ]

Now listen to Track 23 and tick the words and expressions (above) that you hear.

2 **Listen to Track 24 and answer the following questions.**

a   What did Jan do at the age of 19?

   ....

b   Why did she go to a group called *Common Law*?

   ....

c   What three things did she have to do for her audition for *Common Law*?

   ....

d   What story did she tell?

   ....

e   Where did she get the song and game from?

   ....

f   How did she learn the story?

   ....

g   What happened when she told it?

   ....

3 Listen to Track 25. Who or what:

a ... is 'The Spitz'?

....

b ... has a reputation for being late?

....

c ... plays the drums?

....

d ... said he was tired and had to lie down?

....

e ... explained the stories five minutes before the show?

....

f ... was on the edge of creativity?

....

g ... weren't very enthusiastic at first?

....

h ... spoke to the audience to encourage them?

....

i ... had a fantastic experience?

....

4 Look at the audioscript for Tracks 23 and 25 and find Jan's phrases (*a–h*).
What do the phrases in italics mean? What was she talking about in each case?

a *a tried and tested theory*

....

b *Does that make sense?*

....

c something ... *I can't put my finger on*

....

d the opportunity *to delve deep* into your own consciousness

....

e I kind of *went through the sequence of events*

....

f the place was *humming with people*

....

g I asked the audience *to join in*

....

h I'm slightly *off kilter*

....

5 How good is your memory? Without looking back at Activities 1–4, complete the following transcript with one word for each blank.

What are stories for? I (a) .... , I think stories -- this is my (b) ....
opinion. This isn't a (c) .... of tried and tested theory – (d) .... my
personal opinion is (e) .... when someone tells a (f) .... in that arena,
at the (g) .... that the story is being told (h) .... about being human is
(i) .... yeah? The good, the bad. Every (j) .... experience of being
(k) .... is in that room with everybody and it's (l) .... , there's no
judgement of (m) .... it means to be a human (n) .... in that moment.
Does that make sense?
(o) .... what the audience gets from it I think is a (p) .... is held up
and I say to the (q) .... this is us, aren't we great? Or (r) .... we
stupid, or aren't we (s) .... or aren't we vengeful or aren't we (t) ....
lovers or aren't we – this is the whole gamut of (u) .... experience can be
found in a story I think, and I (v) .... that there's something very
fundamental that I (w) .... put my finger on and say what it is.

Now listen to Track 23 again. How many words did you guess correctly?

In an art museum

1 Look at this list of events in the life of the painter Vincent van Gogh.
Listen to Track 26 and put them in the right order.

a Van Gogh meets the painter Paul Gauguin.   ....

b Van Gogh spends time at a mental asylum.   ....

c Van Gogh moves to Arles in southern France.   ....

d Van Gogh slices off a piece of his ear.   ....

e Van Gogh shoots himself.   ....

f Van Gogh goes to live with his brother in Paris.   ....

g Van Gogh spends time in a hospital.   ....

h Van Gogh starts to experiment with new painting techniques.   ....

i Van Gogh becomes a salesman in an art gallery.   ....

j The painter Paul Gauguin joins Van Gogh in Arles.   ....

k Van Gogh studies theology.   ....

2 Look at these two pictures and listen to the descriptions from the museum
audio tour on Track 27. Write the number of the exhibit under the picture.

Exhibit ....   Exhibit ....

3 Listen to Track 27 again and tick whether these statements are true
   or false according to what you hear.

	True	False
a Van Gogh lived in Paris for three years.		
b He had a lot of money at that time.		
c He wanted to try different ways of painting.		
d He did not find the colour grey interesting.		
e He uses the colour red to create a special effect.		
f In the felt hat picture, he is wearing fashionable clothes.		
g Van Gogh never painted other people.		
h A straw hat would not normally be worn with a suit at that time.		
i The main purpose of picture number 28 was to paint a suit.		

4 What do these words and phrases in blue from Track 26 and Track 27 mean here?

a He was a moody young man ...

   ....

b ... became familiar with the new art movements developing at the time.

   ....

c ... scenes of the fields, the peasants and lives typical of the people who lived
   in the countryside.

   ....

d ... he began to use the swirling brush strokes ...

   ....

e ... violent disagreements, culminating in a quarrel ...

   ....

f ... one of his most remarkable paintings, the ominous Crows in the Wheatfields ...

   ....

g The picture is full of varying tones of grey ...

   ....

h The red in his face and particularly in the beard makes the head stand out
   from the background.

   ....

i Van Gogh was always looking for customers for portraits ...

   ....

j ... the range of colours in the jacket, bow-tie and background.

   ....

5 How would you describe one of the two paintings to a blind friend of yours?
   Write your description on a separate piece of paper.

Part B: Speaking

Reading aloud

•••A   Small boy

1   Read the poem and complete the tasks which follow.

Small boy

He picked up a pebble
and threw it in the sea

And another, and another
He couldn't stop

He wasn't trying to fill the sea
He wasn't trying to empty the beach

He was just throwing away
nothing else but

Like a kitten playing
he was practising for the future

when there'll be so many things
he'll want to throw away

if only his fingers will unclench
and let them go

Norman MacCraig

 a Listen to Track 28 and write in the commas and full stops in the
poem, depending on how the speaker reads it.
b Check your version with the audioscript.
c Listen to Track 28 again and read along with the speaker.
d Practise reading the poem.
e Read the poem into a tape recorder. Compare your version with
Track 28.

● B Space Station 5

1 Read the story extract and complete the tasks which follow.

> They had been up here for five years Five years for five people cut off from earth since World War IV True the Moonshuttle came every six months with a supply of food but it was pilotless They had not been able to make contact with Moonbase for two years Cathy said it was weird
>   You say that three times a day Rosie answered
>   Well it's true It's weird and I don't think I can stand it much longer
>   Oh for Jupiter's sake shut up Go and play eight-dimensional death-chess and leave me alone You drive me crazy!
>   You shouldn't have spoken to me like that Cathy said quietly and left the cabin The door hissed behind her

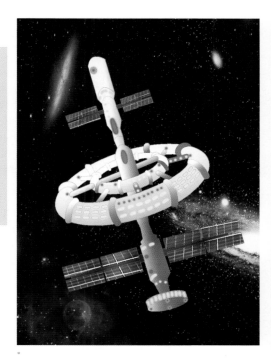

a Listen to Track 29 and write in commas, full stops and inverted commas depending on how the speaker reads it.
b Check your version with the audioscript.
c Listen to Track 29 again and read along with the speaker.
d Practise reading the extract.
e Read the extract into a tape recorder. Compare your version with Track 29.

● C Reading the news (1)

1 Read this transcript of a news broadcast and listen to it on Track 30. Complete the tasks which follow.

> In London today a very unusual story of the perfect crime that went wrong, the bank robbery that failed. Everything seemed to be just right: the timing had been planned to the minute, the escape route was ready, even the hiding place for the money had been carefully prepared. The getaway driver had been handpicked as someone who could be trusted. The robbery went without a hitch and the robber ran out of the bank with over £100,000 in cash. Unfortunately for the robber, Wayne Smith from East London, when he reached the getaway car, his friend the driver, wanting to make the escape as fast as possible, ran him over. Smith and his accomplice are both in hospital tonight where they are reported to be in a stable condition.

a Listen and decide whether the newsreader's voice goes (a) up, (b) down, (c) up and then down or (d) down and then up in the parts in blue.
b Practise saying the news item, paying special attention to the sections in blue in the transcript.
c Read the news item aloud along with the newsreader until you feel you are speaking in a similar fashion to him.

2 Record your news broadcast and compare it with the one on Track 30. You can combine this with the news broadcast in Track 31.

▶ There are more activities related to this news broadcast in Listening 16 on page 42.

D Reading the news (2)

1 Read this transcript of a news broadcast and listen to it on Track 31. Complete the tasks which follow.

> [Some crime news] [from across the Atlantic]. [In Florida today], [Reinero Torres Junior] [was finally prosecuted] [after going to court for a third time]. [The first two times he had been found not guilty] [of the charges of shoplifting from a local store] [and had gone free]. [Today he was finally convicted] [at the third attempt]. [His crime?] [Stealing law books] [from the court house library] [which he was using] [to prepare the defence for his first two cases].

a For each phrase [between square brackets], underline the syllable or syllables that have the strongest stress.
b Check your answers in the answer key.
c Read the news broadcast aloud along with the newsreader on Track 31.

2 Record your news broadcast and compare it with the one on Track 31. You can combine this with the news broadcast on Track 30.

▶ There are more activities related to this news broadcast in Listening 16 on page 42.

E The leisure centre

1 Read the following three paragraphs as if you were recording an automatic message for a telephone answering machine. Try to sound friendly, and give the information in a clear and helpful way.

Use your watch or, better still, a stopwatch, to time yourself.

a

> Welcome to the High Park Leisure Centre. If you know the extension of the person you are calling, please put in that number now. If you would like to become a member of the Centre, please press 2.

b

> If you would like information about our facilities and opening hours, please stay on the line. You may hang up at any time.

c

> The High Park Leisure Centre is your super centre for all types of leisure activities from ice-skating to tennis to swimming. Our opening hours are from 7 am to 10 pm Monday to Friday, 8 am to 10 pm on Saturdays and 10 am to 6 pm on Sundays. We are open every day of the year except 25th December and New Year's Day.

2 Now listen to these three paragraphs on Track 12 (they are the first three paragraphs) and time them using your watch (or better still a stopwatch). Who reads faster, you or the person on Track 12?

3 Listen to Track 12 again. On the transcript on the previous page, underline any words that you will want to stress when you speak the messages again.

4 Read the announcements aloud with the speaker on Track 12. Try and use the same speed, intonation and stress as she uses.

▶ There are more activities related to the High Park Leisure Centre announcement in Listening 7 on page 20.

F Laura

1 Listen to the first part of Track 10. Put a full stop (.) or a comma (,) in the circles. Change the following letters into capital letters, if necessary.

Stop the recording at the end of this extract.

Laura scringed away from the wall ◯ the wolf was on the other side of it ◯ she was too scared to make a sound ◯ the cold was not in her backbone only ◯ it was all through her ◯ Mary pulled the quilt over her head ◯ Jack growled and showed his teeth at the quilt in the doorway ◯ 'be still, Jack ◯ ' Pa said. Terrible howls curled all around the house ◯ and Laura rose out of bed ◯ she wanted to go to Pa ◯ but she knew better than to bother him now ◯ he turned his head and saw her standing in her nightgown. 'Want to see them?' he asked softly ◯ Laura couldn't say anything ◯ but she nodded ◯ and padded across the ground to him ◯ he stood his gun against the wall and lifted her up to the window-hole.

There in the moonlight stood half a circle of wolves ◯ they sat on their haunches and looked at Laura in the window ◯ and she looked at them ◯ she had never seen such big wolves ◯ the biggest one was taller than Laura ◯ he was taller even than Mary ◯ he sat in the middle, exactly opposite Laura ◯ everything about him was big – his pointed ears ◯ and pointed mouth with the tongue hanging out ◯ and his strong shoulders and legs ◯ and his two paws side by side ◯ and his tail curled around the squatting haunch ◯ his coat was shaggy grey and his eyes were glittering green.

Check your answers with the audioscript for Track 10.

2 Look at the extract. If you were going to read it in an American accent like the speaker on Track 10, which words would you find difficult to pronounce? Practise saying the words.

3 Read the passage aloud along with the reader on Track 10. Try and use the same pronunciation, pace and stress and intonation patterns as she does.

▶ There are more activities related to Laura's story in Listening 5 on page 16.

Taking part

•••A Interviewer's questions

1 Read the two conversations and put the interviewer's questions in the appropriate blanks.

- So it wouldn't matter if you didn't play for, say, two weeks?
- Isn't that dangerous?
- Why not? Two weeks isn't a very long time.
- People do get trapped, though, don't they?
- So it's really important to you? You can't live without it?
- Potholing?

Carmen

HUSBAND:	She spends all her time potholing.
a INTERVIEWER:	....
HUSBAND:	Yes. I call it crawling through underground caves on your hands and knees.
b INTERVIEWER:	....
HUSBAND:	Well I think it is and I've begged her to stop but she says she can't. She's obsessed by it and that's the truth.
CARMEN:	It's not that dangerous.
c INTERVIEWER:	....
CARMEN:	Well yes, but I've been potholing for ten years now and I've never had any trouble.

Marcus

MARCUS:	Yes, it's true, I do like playing golf very much.
d INTERVIEWER:	....
MARCUS:	Oh no, I'm not addicted to it or anything. It's something I do just for fun.
e INTERVIEWER:	....
MARCUS:	Two weeks? You can't be serious.
f INTERVIEWER:	....
MARCUS:	Not a long time? You're joking. I begin to feel really unhappy if I don't have a round of golf about twice a week. Oh dear. I suppose that means I am a bit of an addict, doesn't it!

2 Listen to Track 32 and speak Carmen and Marcus' lines. If you need help with your pronunciation, listen to the original conversations on Track 11.

▶ There are more activities related to the interviewer's questions in Listening 6 on page 18.

B Interviewees' replies

1 **Read the two conversations and put the interviewees' answers in the appropriate blanks.**

- And I get a real kick out of it.
- No, not really. Not if you're careful, especially about your equipment.
- No, well it's not for everybody, obviously. But it really turns me on. It still does, even though I've been doing it for four years now. It's just that feeling of surfing the sky, plunging through the air. I just can't get enough of it, frankly.
- Sometimes, a little, but you get that rush of adrenaline, it's just wonderful!
- The only downside is that it can be pretty cold just standing on a station platform all day. They're some of the windiest places on earth.
- Yeah. It's great when you see an engine you've never seen before.

Jack

JACK:	People call us nerds in anoraks, I know, but we aren't doing anybody any harm.
INTERVIEWER:	Well no.
a JACK:	....
INTERVIEWER:	You do?
b JACK:	....
INTERVIEWER:	I'll take your word for it.
c JACK:	....
	....
INTERVIEWER:	Yes, I imagine they are.

Ellie

INTERVIEWER:	Isn't what you do really dangerous?
d ELLIE:	....
INTERVIEWER:	But don't you ever get scared? I know I would be.
e ELLIE:	....
	....
INTERVIEWER:	I don't think I'd be very keen.
f ELLIE:	....
	....

2 **Listen to Track 33 and speak Jack and Ellie's lines. If you need help with your pronunciation, listen to the original conversations on Track 11.**

▶ There are more activities related to these interviews in Listening 6 on page 18.

●●●C Cynic and believer (1)

1 Complete the following utterances with words from the box.

Internet	believed
palms	conversation
sometimes	convinced
stars	crystal balls
university	doing
upside	future
used	horoscope

♈ **Aries** March 21-April 19

♉ **Taurus** April 20-May 20

♊ **Gemini** May 21-June 21

♋ **Cancer** June 22-July 22

♌ **Leo** July 23-August 22

♍ **Virgo**

1 But why? It's all junk. Look I could write you your (**a**) .... now. Let's see. 'You are a person who longs to be happy but (**b**) .... you're sad. You like to shine in (**c**) .... but sometimes it's difficult for you.' How am I (**d**) .... so far?

2 He's an American professor at some (**e**) .... in the USA. I read an interview with him on the (**f**) ....

3 I (**g**) .... to, but that was before I listened to Ray Hyman talking about it.

4 Not really, no. I mean this Hyman guy started reading (**h**) .... when he was a teenager and people really liked it. They (**i**) .... what he had to tell them. But then one day, just for fun he read this woman's palm (**j**) .... down, backwards. And the thing was, the woman was more (**k**) .... than ever that he was telling her really fantastic things about her life and her (**l**) .... I mean it wouldn't have mattered whether he'd used palms, cards, (**m**) .... or tea leaves. All he had to do was make it up.

5 Why not? Look do you believe the stuff in the papers about your (**n**) .... , you know whether you're a Taurus or a Scorpio or Aquarius or Pisces?

- -

2 Now listen to Track 34. When you hear the beep, choose the correct utterance from Activity 1 above. Write the number here.

a ....

b ....

c ....

d ....

e ....

3 Now listen to the first half of Track 14 to check your answer (or look at the answer key). Complete the following tasks.

    a Listen to the track. Stop it after the woman says 'That describes me perfectly'.
    b While you listen, underline any words the man uses which you find difficult to hear or pronounce.
    c Listen to Track 14 again. Pay special attention to the words you underlined.
    d Play Track 14 again. Read the man's words aloud along with the speaker on the track.

4 Go back and play Track 34. Speak the man's words when you hear the beep (you can pause the recording).

    ▸ There are more activities related to *Cynic and believer* in Listening 9 on page 6.

•D Cynic and believer (2)

1 Read the following utterances (*a–i*). Listen to Track 35. When you hear the beep, choose the correct utterance. Write the letter here. The first one is done for you.

    a And people who bend spoons? And people who see flying saucers? Are they all lying?
    b How do you figure that one out?
    c I might.
    d I think you're just a big cynic. I mean what about people who have lived past lives, you know they can remember things from hundreds of years ago even though no one knows anything about those times?
    e No. Well I don't think so.
    f OK mister Clever, what is it?
    g Well if there isn't any mystery in life, where's the fun?
    h You know what I think?
    i You must be pretty unhappy.

1 ...*d*... 2 .... 3 .... 4 .... 5 ....
6 .... 7 .... 8 .... 9 ....

2 Now listen to the second half of Track 14. Start after the man says 'See? It's easy.' Stop Track 14 after the woman says 'Well if there isn't any mystery in life, where's the fun?' Complete the following tasks.

    a While you listen underline any words the woman uses which you find difficult to hear or pronounce.
    b Listen to Track 14 again. Pay special attention to the words you underlined.
    c Play Track 14 again. Read the woman's words along with the speaker on the track.

3 Go back and play Track 35. Speak the woman's words when you hear the beep. Try to do this in the time provided (but you can always pause the recording if you need to).

▸ There are more activities related to *Cynic and believer* in Listening 9 on page 26.

••• E   Eight bad waiter jokes!

1 There are a lot of jokes about restaurants. Read these jokes and decide which one you like best and why.

2 Read the following 'punch-lines' (the punch-line is the last line of a joke – the one that makes people laugh).

a About three or four inches, if you're lucky, madam.   [ ]

b Accidentally! I moved the lettuce and there it was.   [ ]

c Don't worry, madam, it won't shrink.   [ ]

d It looks like it's swimming, sir.   [ ]

e No, sir, I always walk this way.   [ ]

f No, sir, that's a cockroach. The fly is on your steak.   [ ]

g Thanks for your concern, sir, but it's not that hot.   [ ]

h We serve anyone here, madam.   [ ]

Listen to Track 36 and say the appropriate punch-line when you hear the beep. Write the number of the exchange in the brackets.

On your own

●●A The (celebrity) telephone interview

1   **If a journalist rang you and asked you the following questions for a celebrity interview, how would you answer? Make notes in the spaces provided.**

   a How do you relax?

   ....

   b How would you like to be remembered?

   ....

   c If you could change one thing about your appearance, what would it be?

   ....

   d What is the most important lesson life has taught you?

   ....

   e What is your greatest fear?

   ....

   f What is your greatest regret?

   ....

   g What is your most vivid childhood memory?

   ....

   h What makes you happy?

   ....

   i What three words best describe you?

   ....

   j What words or phrases in English do you use most often?

   ....

   k When you were a child, what was your favourite food?

   ....

   l Which living person would you most like to meet?

   ....

   m Who or what is the greatest love of your life?

   ....

   n Who's your favourite person and why?

   ....

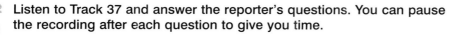

2   **Listen to Track 37 and answer the reporter's questions. You can pause the recording after each question to give you time.**

   Note: the questions are not necessarily in the same order as those above. Not all the questions are used.

B   The job interview

1   Which of the following topics are appropriate for a job interview?
Tick the appropriate boxes.

a why the applicant wants the job   [   ]

b whether the applicant has a girlfriend / boyfriend or is married   [   ]

c how the applicant got on in their last job   [   ]

d what the applicant's favourite colour is   [   ]

e what the applicant does in their spare time   [   ]

f why the applicant thinks that he or she is right for this job   [   ]

g what time the applicant has dinner   [   ]

2   Choose one of the advertisements on page 61, and complete these tasks
using your imagination.

a Give yourself a new name and a fictional CV which would be appropriate
for the job. Write down the main points of the CV.

....

....

....

....

....

b Think of the qualities and experiences that would make the interviewers
like you.

....

....

....

....

c Think of the questions the interviewers are going to ask you and make a
note of some good answers.

....

....

....

....

Train big cats in Las Vegas!

Appear in world-famous circus performances!

Big cats are lions, tigers, cheetahs, etc.

(No experience necessary: we supply on-the-job experience-based training.)

- Fabulous pay
- Fabulous conditions
- An exciting star-studded life

The successful candidate will be:

- energetic
- decisive
- ready for anything
- fit and healthy
- good-humoured
- ambitious

Don't wait! Apply now

Have you ever wanted to write for a popular magazine?

Well now's your chance!

We are looking for someone to write a weekly column in our magazine on any topic they want.

- Excellent pay
- You become well known
- You have influence and people everywhere read your opinions. It's a fantastic opportunity

We provide:

- training
- editorial help
- entertainment allowance (you get a sum of money to spend on going out)

You provide:

- ideas
- imagination
- opinion
- enthusiasm

Volunteers wanted for new TV show

Supreme Challenge ™ will take 15 ordinary members of the public and put them in difficult physical circumstances (on mountains, in the jungle, at sea, etc.).

The winner gets $5m!!!

We are looking for volunteers who are:

brave • cheerful • fit • sociable • good in a crowd • competitive

---

3 Now listen to Track 38 and answer the interviewer's questions about the job you have chosen. You can pause the recording if you have a lot to say for each question.

C Telling a story

1 **Look at the pictures of Mary, her children Jake and Rachael and her husband.**

- Put the pictures in order to tell a story. Start with picture *f*.
- Think about how you would tell the story to a friend. You can make notes, but don't write the whole story down. You can use the words and phrases in the box to help you (check their meaning in a dictionary if you are not sure).
- Practise saying the story either out loud or in your head as many times as you can.
- Record the story on a tape recorder, mini-disk or computer.
- Listen to your story and make notes about how you could improve it.
- Record your story again, using the improvements you have made.

  (You can see a version of the story in the answer key.)

| aisle |
| bucket |
| climbing net |
| commanding officer |
| mop |
| to come to |
| unconscious |

a

b

c

d

e

f

g

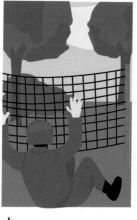

h

i

j

1 *f*   2 _____   3 _____   4 _____   5 _____   6 _____   7 _____   8 _____   9 _____   10 _____

•D Decorating a room

1 You have been asked to decorate a room for students at a college. It is a room where students can hang out, read, have coffee, etc. It is expected that about five people will be in the room at any one time.

Look at the picture of the student room and the items that can go in it.

dining table

chair

armchair

sofa

bookcase

poster

television

stereo system

coffee table

2 Use the space to make notes to answer the following questions.

   a Choose any six items from the furniture list (four chairs count as one item; each armchair is a separate item). What are the reasons for your choices?

   ....

   ....

   ....

   ....

   ....

   ....

   b What colour would you choose for the carpet?

   ....

   c What colour would you choose for the curtains?

   ....

   d What colour would you choose for the walls and the ceiling?

   ....

   e How would you describe the room you have designed to a friend?

   ....

   ....

   ....

   ....

   ....

3 Listen to Track 39. Answer the questions about your room. You can pause the recording after each question to give you time.

••E Making a presentation

1 Complete the following tasks.

   a Choose a hobby or an activity that you would like to talk about, either because you do it just for fun or because you would like to do it.

   b Make notes in answer to the questions on page 65.

Why do you want to talk about it?

What is special about it?

Have you ever done it and what was it like?

OR Would you like to do it and why?

What kind of person does this activity?

When and where is the best place or time to do it?

Who is the best person to do it with?

What would you say to encourage other people to do it?

What does it feel like?

What else would you like to say about it?

2 Use your notes from Activity 1 to plan your talk. You can follow this outline plan.

What you're going to talk about and why

What it is

- what it's like – how does it make you feel?
- how you do it
- how often you do it
- where you do it, etc.

Conclusions

- your last words about it
- why other people should try it, etc.

3 Practise giving your presentation, using your notes. Try not to read them out.

4 Record your presentation. Listen back to it and make a note of any pronunciation problems that you had.

5 Record your presentation again.

F A survey

1 Read the following 'brief' for a survey.

You have been asked to conduct a street survey about people and eating. The focus of the survey is on 'eating out' – that is, going to restaurants. That could mean fast food like hamburgers that you can buy anywhere on the street, railway stations, etc., to more expensive restaurants.

The survey organisers have asked you to find out information about the following things:

- how often people eat out.

- where they eat out (street stall, fast-food restaurant, pizzeria, gourmet restaurant, etc.)

- what kind of food they like to eat when they eat out.

- what they want from a restaurant (speed and efficiency, good service, etc.)

- what would stop them going to a restaurant.

2   Design your survey. Pay attention to the following points.

- the information you want to find out
  (you can divide your survey into sections)
- the questions you will ask
- the language you will use – look at the way
  the following words and phrases are used
  in the audioscript for Track 16.

friendly service	lots of variety
get served quickly	on the menu
good food	plain food
great value	soft lighting
home-cooked food	spicy
hygienic	the right atmosphere

3   Write out your questionnaire. Practise saying the questions.

4   Record your survey questions. You can start by saying 'Good morning,
sir / madam. I wonder if you would mind answering a few questions …'.
Listen back to them and make a note of any problems you had.

5   Record your survey questions again. Now you can interview yourself!
Stop your recording after each question to give appropriate answers.

Speaking and writing

●●●A Ellipsis

1 In writing, we generally make complete questions and sentences.
In informal speech, however, we often leave out all but the most important words.

Examples: 'Nice day!' instead of 'Isn't it a nice day?' or 'It's a nice day, isn't it?'
'Coffee?' instead of 'Would you like a coffee?'
'Raining.' instead of 'It's raining.'

2 What might be the full (written) form for A's utterances in the following exchanges?

a A: Surprised? ....
B: Yes, just a bit.

b A: Difficult exam? ....
B: No, not too bad.

c A: Biscuit? ....
B: No thanks. I've just eaten.

d A: Nice car. ....
B: Thanks. Glad you like it.

e A: Going to rain. ....
B: Yes, I think you're right.

f A: Drink? ....
B: Yes, let's.

g A: Starting a new job tomorrow. ....
B: You're doing what?

h A: Hot! ....
B: Yes it is.

3 Where do you think the conversations in Activity 2 might have taken place?

a ....

b ....

c ....

d ....

e ....

f ....

g ....

h ....

•B Speaking–like and writing–like

1 Are the following phrases, sentences and questions more writing-like
or speaking-like? Write *W*, *S*, or *W / S* if they can be both in the brackets.

a Fantastic, aren't they?   [   ]
b I think they are fantastic.   [   ]
c CU L8R.   [   ]
d See you later.   [   ]
e I was like 'fine' and he was like 'OK'.   [   ]
f I said that it was fine and he replied that it was OK.   [   ]
g I'm not going to put up with it anymore.   [   ]
h I'm not going to tolerate it any more.   [   ]
i You're not from round here, are you?   [   ]
j Do you come from this neighbourhood?   [   ]
k You're a gambler?   [   ]
l Are you a gambler?   [   ]
m Check out the new cafeteria! Awesome!   [   ]
n It is worth investigating the new cafeteria.   [   ]

•C Speaking–like and writing–like

1 Match the phrases in italics in sentences *a–l* with their meanings (*1–12*).

a *Believe it or not* they've just got married.
b *I don't believe a word of it.*
c *It's difficult to see the point of* the film.
d Justice must be done and *must be seen to be done.*
e *Let's see how it goes,* shall we?
f *See you later.*
g *Seen from this distance* the events of 1973 are difficult to understand.
h *She sees herself as* the leader of the group.
i The cinema? *I don't see why not.*
j The moment he finishes his course *you won't see him for dust.*
k When they saw the spaceship *they could scarcely believe their eyes.*
l You want your car fixed? *I'll see what I can do.*

1 Goodbye.
2 He'll leave immediately.
3 I don't understand why the film was made.
4 I know it sounds ridiculous, but …
5 I'll do my best.
6 It must be clear that everything is being done fairly.
7 It's just not possible.
8 They were very surprised.
9 She thinks of herself as number 1.
10 We'll try and deal with any problems if and when they arise.
11 When we consider something a long time after the event …
12 Yes, that seems like a good suggestion.

a …………   b …………   c …………   d …………   e …………   f …………
g …………   h …………   i …………   j …………   k …………   l …………

2 Look at the sentences *a–l* in the previous activity on page 69. Pay special attention to the phrases in italics.

Write *F* for 'formal', *I* for 'informal', *Conv.* for 'more likely to be heard in conversation', or *W* for 'more likely to be seen in writing' for each one.

a ....

b ....

c ....

d ....

e ....

f ....

g ....

h ....

i ....

j ....

k ....

l ....

●●● D When words are used

1 Some words are much more common in spoken English than in written English – or vice versa.

Look at the dictionary entries from the *Longman Dictionary of Contemporary English*.
Are the words used more in spoken or in written English, according to the dictionary makers?
Write *S* or *W* in the blanks.

fan·cy¹ [S3] /'fænsi/ *v* fancied, fancying, fancies [T]
1 LIKE/WANT *BrE informal* to like or want something, or want to do something; ⊟ feel like: *Fancy a quick drink, Emma?* | **fancy doing sth** *Sorry, but I don't fancy going out tonight.*
2 SEXUAL ATTRACTION *BrE informal* to feel sexually attracted to someone: *All the girls fancied him.*
3 fancy yourself *BrE informal* to behave in a way that shows you think you are very attractive or clever: *That bloke on the dance floor really fancies himself.*
4 fancy yourself (as) sth *BrE* to believe, usually wrongly, that you have particular skills or are a particular type

a ....

fright·ened [S2] /'fraɪtnd/ *adj* feeling afraid; ⊟ scared: *Don't be frightened. We're not going to hurt you.* | [+of] *I was frightened of being left by myself in the house.* | *Her father had an awful temper and she was always frightened of him.* | **frightened to do sth** *The boy was frightened to speak.* | **frightened that** *She's frightened that her ex-husband will find her.* | *To tell the truth, I was **frightened to death** (=very frightened).* | *a frightened horse* ⚠ Do not confuse **frightened**, which describes a feeling, and **frightening**, which describes something that makes you feel frightened: *a frightened child* | *a frightening experience;* → see box at FEAR¹

b ....

favour² [W3] *BrE;* **favor** *AmE v* [T]
1 PREFER to prefer someone or something to other things or people, especially when there are several to choose from: *Both countries seem to favour the agreement.* | *loose clothing of the type favoured in Arab countries* | **favour sb/sth over sb/sth** *Florida voters favored Bush over Gore by a very small margin.*
2 GIVE AN ADVANTAGE to treat someone much better than someone else, in a way that is not fair: *a tax cut that favours rich people* | **favour sb over sb** *a judicial system that favours men over women*
3 HELP to provide suitable conditions for something

c ....

fre·quent¹ [W3] /'friːkwənt/ *adj* happening or doing something often; ⊟ infrequent: **more/less frequent** *Her headaches are becoming less frequent.* | *Trains rushed past at frequent intervals.* | *She was a frequent visitor to the house.*

d ....

E Reporting conversations and events

1 **In the following pairs, which sentence is more formal or writing-like, 1 or 2?**
Which sentence is more informal or conversation-like, 1 or 2? Write *F* or *I* on the line.

a **1** He's like 'that's cool' and I'm like 'well yeah!' ....

2 He said that it was cool and I replied that it was. ....

b **1** So she goes 'that's ridiculous' and then goes red in the face. ....

2 She said that it was ridiculous and then she went red in the face. ....

c **1** So this guy he asks me where I'm going and I'm like 'why do you want to know?' ....

2 A man asked me where I was going and I asked him why he wanted to know. ....

d **1** So he's like about to completely lose it and I'm like 'calm down, OK' and he's like 'thanks, I needed that.' ....

2 He was about to lose control and so I suggested that he calmed down and he thanked me. ....

e **1** We say 'hello' and they go 'what are you guys doing here?' and we go 'well you asked us, didn't you?' ....

2 We said 'hello' and they asked us what we were doing there. We said that they'd invited us. ....

2 **Find examples of *to be like* and *go(es)* in sentences in Activity 1. Now write *to be like* and / or *go(es)* in the blanks.**

a It is used for reporting conversations. ....

b It is informal and used when talking. ....

c It is used mainly in British English. ....

d It is an informal phrase, used especially in American English. ....

F Redundancy, hesitation and direction change

1 **Look at this transcript of an extract from Track 19. Read it while you listen to that section of Track 19, and then complete the tasks which follow.**

Oooh you feel numb. The ... you know it's it's a saturation point. It's too much for you to digest that your grin is stuck on your face. It was stuck on my face for weeks. I would position that crown in such a way that as soon as I opened my eyes I would see my crown. I did that for weeks. Ha ha. It was such a great feeling. You just you're just grinning and you are just numb. If that's what euphoria is, you know, umm you you can't speak very clearly. You speak but you're just so excited you're tripping over your own words, and immediately there was a press conference on stage itself and it's like ooh ooh ooh because you go from being nobody, a regular person. That's not fair. It's not a nobody. You go from being a regular person to being in every newspaper around the world and everyone knows. It went from going in a bus with 87 other girls to 'and Miss World 1997 is Miss India' to a stretch limousine, with bodyguards, where the heads of the company moved out of the presidential suite and I took over and chaperones and that's what it was right since then. You sit in the cockpits for take-offs and landings. You're treated like a queen you, you know, you have private planes, and all these flights and umm the red carpet and it's just Lights! Camera! Action!

a Find as many examples as possible where Diana repeats words or phrases. Why does she do this?

b Find as many examples as you can where Diana uses 'meaningless' sounds to help her pause. Why does she do this?

c Find examples where Diana changes the grammatical construction of a sentence after she has actually started it.

d Take two sentences which have the features you found for items *a–c*. Rewrite them as if Diana was writing about her experiences for a magazine article (i.e. without the spoken features you have identified).

2 **Look at the audioscript for the track numbers below. Analyse them in the same way. Rewrite sentences as you did in *d* above.**

Track numbers: 6, 7, 8, 18, 23, 24, 25

AUDIOSCRIPT

Track 1

SUZANNE: Hello Don. I'm Suzanne Moore, your financial advisor. How may I help you, Don?

DON: I guess I just need some general help with money. My biggest problem is that I never seem to have any. I just don't know where it goes. I'm not a big spendthrift, but I just can't seem to make ends meet.

SUZANNE: I see. I'm sure I can help you with that. Now, tell me Don – do you have a job at all?

DON: Yeah – well, I'm an English Lit. major so I have a lot of work, but I work every afternoon at Pauline's Pizza. I don't think it's enough, but if I, if I work any more I won't have time to study.

SUZANNE: Hmm – that's a dilemma, isn't it? Here's the first thing you need to do. You're going to have to make a budget so that you can control your finances better.

DON: What do you mean?

SUZANNE: It's easy – just take a piece of paper and write down everything you spend money on – food, rent, books, going out, music, whatever you spend your money on – your expenditure. And then on the other side, you write down what you could change and cut down on to save money.

DON: OK – I think I can do that. It sounds like a good idea.

Track 2

SUZANNE: OK. Let's try it. How much money do you spend on groceries per week?

DON: Hmm. It varies from one week to the next, but I'd guess about $100.

SUZANNE: OK, that seems like rather a lot.

DON: Well, I usually go to the local store about four times a week and spend about $25.

SUZANNE: There's your first problem. Try to go to markets – they often have good prices and specials. Perhaps you could go just once a week to a market. You should be able to cut your food bills in half.

DON: Sounds like a good idea.

SUZANNE: What about rent? How much do you spend on rent?

DON: $500. I share a place with two other people. It's a cool place – we each have our own rooms and we have a nice common area and a great kitchen.

SUZANNE: Hmm. You could find something cheaper, but it might not be as nice. You'll have to think about that.

DON: OK. I think I don't want to do that.

SUZANNE: What about going out and entertainment?

DON: Well, I buy a couple of CDs every week.

SUZANNE: You could cut back to one.

DON: I go to the movies once a week.

SUZANNE: Make it once every two weeks. What about eating out?

DON: I eat in the school cafeteria most days.

SUZANNE: Why not make your own food instead? Make yourself a sandwich at home. It's much cheaper – and try to share the expenses with your roommates.

DON: They cook worse than I do, but I guess we could all work on it.

SUZANNE: See. These are just a few tips to help you save a little money.

DON: Yeah, thanks, Suzanne. I may even be able to make a little investment for my future.

SUZANNE: That's a good idea – you're never too young to start thinking about an investment. Perhaps we can talk about that sometime soon ...

Track 3

Er ... So this woman gets on a bus for the start of a long journey from Paris to London. She soon finds out that the man she's sitting next to is a talker – he just won't shut up. And she just wants to sleep for the whole journey so she's a bit disappointed. The guy keeps asking her questions and then, to make matters worse, he turns to her and asks her if she'd like to play a game. She says 'No, thank you' as politely as she can and closes her eyes to go to sleep, hoping he'll get the message.

Track 4

WOMAN: ... to make matters worse he turns to her and asks her if she'd like to play a game. She says 'No, thank you' as politely as she can and closes her eyes to go to sleep, hoping he'll get the message.

But the man is not put off easily and he insists, saying that the game will be fun and that it's very easy. Even though she couldn't care less, he tells her the rules. 'I'll ask you a question and if you don't know the answer you have to pay me £5 and then you'll ask me a question and if I don't know the answer I have to pay you £5.'

The woman can't believe her bad luck. This is the last thing she wants to do, so again she says that she's not interested and turns away from him to try to get to sleep. The man is getting more and more frustrated and desperate to play by this time, so he decides to change the rules to see if that will tempt her. 'OK,' he says, 'if you don't know the answer you only have to pay me £1 and if I don't know the answer, I'll pay you £20.'

So, the woman analyses the situation and comes to the conclusion that the only way to get some sleep is to play this ridiculous game, so she finally agrees to the game. So as you can imagine, the man is all keen when he asks the first question: 'How far is it around the earth?'. The woman doesn't say a word – she just reaches into her handbag, takes out £1 and gives it to the man.

So now it's the woman's turn. She looks him right in the eyes and says, 'What's green in the morning, blue in the afternoon and red in the evening?'. The man looks shocked. He thought this was going to be a piece of cake for him – what could this woman possibly know that he doesn't know? He gets on his mobile phone and calls all his friends, gets on the Internet using his phone and searches every reference he can, but still can't get the answer. He sends e-mails to famous professors, but no one knows the answer.

Finally, after a couple of hours he wakes the woman (who's been sleeping soundly all this time) and admits to being beaten. 'I don't know the answer!' he whispers, weeping with despair. 'Here's your £20'. Without a word, the woman takes the money and puts it in her bag and goes straight back to sleep. So, the man is completely flabbergasted and through his tears he wakes her and begs for the answer. 'Please put me out of my misery,' he pleads, 'what's the answer?' The woman reaches into her bag and gives him a pound.

Track 5

Peter

I took this picture when I was about ten, I think. My parents had taken me to a place called Arosa in Switzerland. They'd decided to learn how to ski. It was quite a surprise I think because before that we'd only ever been on holiday in England. We used to go to the seaside every summer. But this winter, for some reason, well I don't know. Anyway, they'd given me this box camera for Christmas. Box cameras were just that, a little box with a funny little viewfinder to look through, and film, quite big, which is funny considering you got such small prints!

I loved skiing and the snow. D'you know I think it was my first time abroad ever. But all that fresh mountain air and racing down the slopes. It was really great. Fantastic. I haven't been skiing for years. I've probably forgotten how to.

I wonder what happened to that box camera. It was so primitive compared to the digital ones you get nowadays.

Jane

I really love this picture. It's me and my sister on the old Inca trail, you know, in Peru. Well it's something I'd always wanted to do, and then when my sister spent a few months in Chile between school and university I went out and joined her. It was one of the best trips I've ever done. We went up through Chile, then Bolivia and into Peru. Like everyone who goes to South America we wanted to see the fabulous old Inca city of Machu Picchu, so we travelled to Cuzco which is the old capital of the Inca empire, you know before the Spaniards got there in the 16th century and started their 300-year rule in that part of the world. Well not 300 years exactly. Anyway, so you leave Cuzco and walk the Inca trail. It's spectacular scenery. And then, when you get to Machu Picchu itself, well it's absolutely fantastic, just as good as everyone says and much much better than any photograph you've ever seen of it. There are places like that aren't there, you know, no matter how often you've seen photographs it's just not a patch on the real thing. Machu Picchu was like that.

Kate

Oh yeah, that's the Grand Palace in Bangkok. In Thailand. It's a fantastic place. I mean, I haven't been in Thailand for ten years, but I can remember it really well. I loved Bangkok better than some of the other places. Well I can hardly remember Egypt cos I was just a kid then, and I didn't specially like the school I was in in Johannesburg when we were there. But Thailand. Thailand was really cool.

My dad was a diplomat – well he still is – and my Mom's a teacher. That's why we lived in so many different places.

The Grand Palace dates back to the 18th century, I think. That's when King Rama I had it built. See, I really paid attention to all that stuff. I think I remember it correctly anyway. It's a fantastic place. There are temples and pagodas and some incredible wall paintings. I went there quite a few times. Well every time friends or family would come out to visit we'd take them to different places, you know, kind of like tourist guides cos we knew what to show them, and at the palace they'd be like 'wow! that's fabulous!'.

I'd so like to go back to Bangkok and see some of my friends there. Maybe I will next vacation. Maybe.

Betty

Oh no, look at that! That's me and my dog Sally … well, and my sister, of course. I wonder how old I was then. I must have been, what, about six or seven. I loved that dog. We went everywhere together. Well, in my memory we did anyway. I used to take her over the fields to my friend's house, and in the summer she'd come with us on long walks when we went on holidays. We used to go to this farm in the hills. I loved that, so did my brothers. We used to have a fantastic time.

And Sally! D'you know I haven't thought about her for years. I loved that dog. And then when I was about 11, they sent me away to school and the dog passed away. I was heartbroken. It was so difficult being young back then. A lot easier now, I can tell you.

Track 6

INTERVIEWER: Why are you called Hag?

HAG: Er because my surname is Hargreaves, Ian James Hargreaves, and when I was seven, six or seven at school, from Hargreaves you got Haggis, Hargreaves Haggis, which was shortened to Hag, simple as that and I kept it, because I don't like Ian.

INTERVIEWER: And you've been Hag ever since?

HAG: I've been Hag ever since but when I went to college I had to carry it with me of course because people started calling me Ian and I hated being called Ian because the only people who called me Ian were teachers or parents …

INTERVIEWER: And Hag then became your professional name as well?

HAG: It did, yeah everyone knows me as Hag, apart from a couple of annoying people.

Track 7

HAG: I suppose, broadly speaking, I'm an illustrative photographer er in that I illustrate ideas by putting images together, by putting, you know several negatives into the same picture, usually to make a coherent image rather than an abstract image although I have been working with abstract ideas recently.

INTERVIEWER: Can you give an example in words of the kind of thing you're talking about?

HAG: Er, well the one that immediately comes to mind is 'a storm in a teacup', er which is exactly what it says it is. It's a storm in a teacup but of course the storm in the teacup is actually a storm that is put in the teacup and the teacup's surrounded by a storm, so this makes a storm in a teacup.

INTERVIEWER: And this is a number of different photographs blended into one?

HAG: Yes, five I think, four, four or five. It's done in a darkroom. I have, if I, I have got eight enlargers. It's like having a multi-track recording studio if you like. I've got eight enlargers. Put a negative in each enlarger and print the bit of the negative you need onto the same piece of paper and then move to the next enlarger and print the next bit you want onto that same piece of paper so you end up with an image that's, all the elements are printed from the original negative. There's no copying involved or anything. It's just a question of masking it right so they fit together perfectly.

INTERVIEWER: You make it sound very simple, but it isn't simple at all is it?

HAG: Aah. No. It isn't simple at all. It's just, you have to be patient. You have to understand a few things.

INTERVIEWER: Who likes your combination pictures?

HAG: I don't know (laughs). People like them. I've sold hundreds and thousands of pictures throughout the world in posters and postcards and things. And people have bought these with their own money. It's not like an art director in an agency you know thinks 'I want to employ this trendy photographer'. They actually have to put their hands, they have to walk into a shop, they have to like it, they have to put their hands in their pocket and buy it with their own money and that's very flattering.

INTERVIEWER: Because there've been one or two have been very very successful posters, haven't they?

HAG: There's been, yes, yes, I've had some very successful posters er, unfortunately the most successful one I don't really like it just being a dolphin picture, some dolphins leaping out of the water, that was made into all sorts of things like er duvet covers and pillowcase sets, watches, clocks, jigsaw puzzle, er there are other th- apart from the posters and cards and postcards. Yes, that kept me alive for a few years.

Track 8

HAG: When I moved four years ago and built a new darkroom which took me all summer and was a terrible struggle, people said to me 'Hag, why are you bothering building a darkroom? Do it on a computer.' My answer was, well there's two answers. Firstly I'm not Hag without a darkroom. I have to have a darkroom. Doesn't matter whether I use it or not but it has to be there. I don't feel whole without it. The second answer these questions, often come up while sitting in a restaurant eating a meal in candlelight. Now when were candles redundant, when were they obsolete technologically? You know, 200 years ago? And there we are, we're still sitting around a table eating meals with candlelight because it's nice, because they have a certain quality that you cannot get anywhere else except by a naked flame and that live flame on the table has a certain essence that you do not get from a light-bulb. So we use the technologies, we use the tools for the qualities they have. A computer does not produce an original hand-made print that's printed from the … from each element er on to that piece of paper. Now people will pay for that rather than buying a digital file that's been created on a computer and then printed, no matter how well. It is not the same thing, it is a reproduction of a digital file.
INTERVIEWER: So film isn't going to go away?
HAG: No.

Track 9

Suddenly, she was sitting straight up in bed. She had been asleep. The dark was gone. Moonlight streamed through the window-hole and streaks of moonlight came through every crack in the wall. Pa stood black in the moonlight at the window. He had his gun. Right in Laura's ear a wolf howled.

Track 10

Laura scringed away from the wall. The wolf was on the other side of it. She was too scared to make a sound. The cold was not in her backbone only, it was all through her. Mary pulled the quilt over her head. Jack growled and showed his teeth at the quilt in the doorway.

'Be still, Jack,' Pa said.

Terrible howls curled all around the house, and Laura rose out of bed. She wanted to go to Pa, but she knew better than to bother him now. He turned his head and saw her standing in her nightgown.

'Want to see them?' he asked softly. Laura couldn't say anything, but she nodded, and padded across the ground to him. He stood his gun against the wall and lifted her up to the window-hole.

There in the moonlight stood half a circle of wolves. They sat on their haunches and looked at Laura in the window, and she looked at them. She had never seen such big wolves. The biggest one was taller than Laura. He was taller even than Mary. He sat in the middle, exactly opposite Laura. Everything about him was big – his pointed ears, and pointed mouth with the tongue hanging out, and his strong shoulders and legs, and his two paws side by side, and his tail curled around the squatting haunch. His coat was shaggy grey and his eyes were glittering green.

Laura lifted her toes into a crack in the wall and she folded her arms on the window slab, and she looked and looked at that wolf. But she did not put her head through the empty window space into the outdoors where all those wolves sat so near her,

shifting their paws and licking their chops. Pa stood firm against her back and kept his arm tight round her middle.

'He's awful big,' Laura whispered.

'Yes, and see how his coat shines,' Pa whispered into her hair. The moonlight made little glitters in the edges of the shaggy fur, all around the big wolf.

'They are in a ring clear round the house,' Pa whispered. Laura pattered beside him to the other window. He leaned his gun against that wall and lifted her up again. There, sure enough, was the other half of the circle of wolves. All their eyes glittered green in the shadow of the house. Laura could hear their breathing. When they saw Pa and Laura looking out, the middle of the circle moved back a little way.

After a moment Pa went back to the other window, and Laura went too. They were just in time to see the big wolf lift his nose till it pointed straight at the sky. His mouth opened, and a long howl rose towards the moon.

Then all around the house the circle of wolves pointed their noses towards the sky and answered him. Their howls shuddered through the house and filled the moonlight and quavered away across the vast silence of the prairie.

'Now go back to bed, little half-pint,' Pa said. 'Go to sleep. Jack and I will take care of you all.'

So Laura went back to bed. But for a long time she did not sleep. She lay and listened to the breathing of the wolves on the other side of the log wall. She heard the scratch of their claws on the ground, and the snuffling of a nose at a crack. She heard the big grey leader howl again, and the others answering him.

But Pa was walking quietly from one window-hole to the other and Jack did not stop pacing up and down before the quilt that hung in the doorway. The wolves might howl, but they could not get in while Pa and Jack were there. So at last, Laura fell asleep.

Track 11

Danny

DANNY: When I'm not at school I like to go fishing.
INTERVIEWER: Fishing?
DANNY: Yeah. I'm an angler. Like my Dad.
INTERVIEWER: Isn't that a bit boring?
DANNY: How do you mean?
INTERVIEWER: Well I don't know, you see people sitting by the river for hours without catching anything. I mean just doing nothing.
DANNY: That's why I like it. It gives you time to think.

Carmen

HUSBAND: She spends all her time potholing.
INTERVIEWER: Potholing?
HUSBAND: Yes. I call it crawling through underground caves on your hands and knees.
INTERVIEWER: Isn't that dangerous?
HUSBAND: Well I think it is and I've begged her to stop but she says she can't. She's obsessed by it and that's the truth.
CARMEN: It's not that dangerous.
INTERVIEWER: People do get trapped, though, don't they?
CARMEN: Well yes, but I've been potholing for ten years now and I've never had any trouble.

Jack

JACK: People call us nerds in anoraks, I know, but we aren't doing anybody any harm.
INTERVIEWER: Well, no.
JACK: And I get a real kick out of it.
INTERVIEWER: You do?
JACK: Yeah. It's great when you see an engine you've never seen before.
INTERVIEWER: I'll take your word for it.

JACK: The only downside is that it can be pretty cold just standing on a station platform all day. They're some of the windiest places on earth.

INTERVIEWER: Yes, I imagine they are.

Marcus

MARCUS: Yes it's true, I do like playing golf very much.

INTERVIEWER: So it's really important to you? You can't live without it?

MARCUS: Oh no, I'm not addicted to it or anything. It's something I do just for fun.

INTERVIEWER: So it wouldn't matter if you didn't play for, say, two weeks?

MARCUS: Two weeks? You can't be serious.

INTERVIEWER: Why not? Two weeks isn't a very long time.

MARCUS: Not a long time? You're joking. I begin to feel really unhappy if I don't have a round of golf about twice a week. Oh dear. I suppose that means I am a bit of an addict, doesn't it!

Ellie

INTERVIEWER: Isn't what you do really dangerous?

ELLIE: No, not really. Not if you're careful, especially about your equipment.

INTERVIEWER: But don't you ever get scared? I know I would be.

ELLIE: Sometimes, a little, but you get that rush of adrenaline, it's just wonderful.

INTERVIEWER: I don't think I'd be very keen.

ELLIE: No, well it's not for everybody, obviously. But it really turns me on. It still does, even though I've been doing it for four years now. It's just that feeling of surfing the sky, plunging through the air. I just can't get enough of it, frankly.

Track 12

Welcome to the High Park Leisure Centre. If you know the extension of the person you are calling, please put in that number now. If you would like to become a member of the Centre, please press 2.

If you would like information about our facilities and opening hours, please stay on the line. You may hang up at any time.

The High Park Leisure Centre is your super centre for all types of leisure activities from ice-skating to tennis to swimming. Our opening hours are from 7 am to 10 pm Monday to Friday, 8 am to 10 pm on Saturdays and 10 am to 6 pm on Sundays. We are open every day of the year except the 25th of December and New Year's Day.

The Polar Bear ice-skating rink is open from the beginning of October to the end of April.

The High Park swimming pool is open all year round and costs £3.50 or £1 for members of the High Park Leisure Centre. If you'd also like to use the gym when you come to swim, there is a special price of £5 which allows you all-day access to these facilities.

In the sports centre, tennis, badminton and squash courts are available for rent when the High Park teams do not have matches. Please call 01 800 6767 extension 54 for details of availability and prices.

High Park Leisure Centre classes run all year round and the new winter sessions begin soon on the 15th January. This term we will be offering classes in aerobics, ballet, modern dance, modern jazz, judo, tae kwondo and tai chi. Our classes last for ten weeks. Please take advantage of our online booking service at www.highparkleisurecentre.co.uk to register for a class or to consult our full catalogue of classes. You can also pick up a catalogue at the Centre during our opening hours and special discounts are only available from our office when you register in person. Unfortunately we cannot take registration for classes over the phone.

That concludes this recorded information service. If you would like to hear this information again, please press 1. If you would like to speak to a Leisure Centre representative, please press 3. Thank you for calling the High Park Leisure Centre, your super centre for leisure and entertainment. Goodbye.

Track 13

RADIO ANNOUNCER: Good afternoon and welcome to our second programme called 'How do people learn'. The speaker is Professor Randy Onnix, head of Applied Linguistics at the University of Hameltown.

ONNIX: As I said last week, many people have tried to explain how we learn things, like how to drive, how to play a musical instrument, or how to speak a foreign language. There are many different theories for this, of course, and people are coming up with new ideas every day.

One of the most popular theories in the first half of the 20th century was called behaviourism, and its influence is still felt 100 years on. Indeed, I would go so far as to say that the central tenets of behaviourism are still present in much teaching and learning that goes on today.

The theory of behaviourism is this: if you make someone do something and give them a prize, a reward when they do it correctly, and if you do this again and again and again, then they'll learn to do it every time, and once they have learnt to do it in this way it will, in the end, no longer be necessary to give them that prize. The whole theory of behaviourism, in other words, depends on habit formation – that is getting people so habituated to a task that they do it without thinking.

Now, there are many examples of this type of habit formation. The Russian researcher Pavlov, for example, taught his dogs that the sound of a bell ringing meant that they were going to be given food. As a result, every time he rang the bell the dogs salivated – even, in the end, when there was no food. Then there were all the experiments with rats. When the rats saw a light, they had to press a bar in their cages. When they pressed the bar they got some food. They did it again and again and again. In the end they learnt to press the bar *every time* they saw the light.

But perhaps my favourite example of this kind of experiment happened in the United States way back in 1920. Two researchers, called Watson and Raynor, experimented on a young boy who had a beautiful pet rabbit. Watson and Raynor wanted to see if they could train Albert to feel differently about his rabbit and so every time he went near the animal they made a terrible noise and, quite naturally, little Albert became frightened. They did this again and again until the poor boy developed a phobia, first just about rabbits, then about animals in general and finally anything with fur. Every time Albert came face to face with an animal or a fur coat, he'd start to show symptoms of terrible fear, crying, feeling sick and feeling faint.

Watson and Raynor were really pleased! 'This just shows that our theory works!' they said. Then they talked to Albert's parents. 'Can we go on with the experiment?' they asked. 'We can turn it round and make Albert love rabbits again.' But Albert's parents told them, for some reason, to go away!

Watson and Raynor's experiment sounds absolutely terrible to us today, but the idea of conditioning is still around. If people do the same thing enough times and get continual encouragement (or discouragement), the doing of it will become automatic – they will be able to do it without thinking.

Not all learning is the result of conditioning though. Other researchers have said that intelligence and creativity matter too. But that's the subject of my next talk. Until then, goodbye.

Track 14

WOMAN: Do you believe in the paranormal, you know, fortune-telling, astrology, past lives, etc.?

MAN: I used to, but that was before I listened to Ray Hyman talking about it.

WOMAN: Who's he?

MAN: He's an American professor at some university in the USA. I read an interview with him on the Internet.

WOMAN: So you don't believe in that stuff now?

MAN: Not really, no. I mean this Hyman guy started reading palms when he was a teenager and people really liked it. They believed what he had to tell them. But then one day, just for fun, he read this woman's palm upside down, backwards. And the thing was, the woman was more convinced than ever that he was telling her really fantastic things about her life and her future. I mean it wouldn't have mattered whether he'd used palms, cards, crystal balls or tea leaves. All he had to do was make it up.

WOMAN: Oh come on, you're not saying all that is complete rubbish?

MAN: Why not? Look, do you believe the stuff in the papers about your stars, you know whether you're a Taurus or a Scorpio or Aquarius or Pisces?

WOMAN: Well yes, I read my stars all the time.

MAN: But why? It's all junk. Look, I could write you your horoscope now. Let's see. 'You are a person who longs to be happy but sometimes you're sad. You like to shine in conversation but sometimes it's difficult for you.' How am I doing so far?

WOMAN: Fine. That describes me perfectly.

MAN: OK, then let's go on. 'You sometimes don't get the love you think you need, but next week you should concentrate all your efforts on someone near to you.'

WOMAN: Well, I have been worrying about my mother. I haven't been ...

MAN: See? It's easy.

WOMAN: I think you're just a big cynic. I mean, what about people who have lived past lives, you know they can remember things from hundreds of years ago even though no one knows anything about those times.

MAN: Well there's an explanation.

WOMAN: OK mister Clever, what is it?

MAN: I don't know. But there's always an explanation. There isn't any mystery out there.

WOMAN: And people who bend spoons? And people who see flying saucers? Are they all lying?

MAN: Not exactly. They're not lying, no. They're often trying to make sense of a chaotic confusing world. And we're all susceptible to suggestion.

WOMAN: How do you figure that one out?

MAN: Well suppose you saw a headline saying 'baby is a space alien'. You wouldn't believe it, would you?

WOMAN: No. Well I don't think so.

MAN: But suppose you kept seeing it in different papers, heard it on shows, heard it from the mouths of people you trusted. You'd believe it then, perhaps?

WOMAN: I might.

MAN: Well there you are.

WOMAN: You know what I think?

MAN: No what?

WOMAN: You must be pretty unhappy.

MAN: Why?

WOMAN: Well if there isn't any mystery in life, where's the fun?

MAN: But there is a mystery!

WOMAN: Oh yes. What?

MAN: I don't know what you would say if I asked you a question.

WOMAN: What question?

MAN: If I asked you whether you were going to eat all that pizza yourself or give me some, what would your answer be?

WOMAN: Well now, that depends.

MAN: On what?

WOMAN: On whether you are prepared to admit that not everything is as easy to explain as you say.

MAN: Well, I am rather hungry ...

Track 15

INSTRUCTOR: Well now, Mr ... er ... Radinski, have you ever driven a car before? ... You have? ... On your father's farm ... but you crashed into the gate and it had to be repaired ... and the radiator needs replacing because you drove into a wall ... and your father is buying some new wing mirrors because you drove too close to the fence ... how interesting ... yes, I hope it will be easier now too, Mr Radinski.

Right, let's start ... OK? ... Adjust your rear-view mirror ... good ... and what about your wing mirrors? Where? You see that button there, do you see? Yes, that one ... excellent ... Now make sure the car is in neutral ... yes, that's right. Now switch on the engine ... that's good ... Er, you can take your foot off the accelerator now, Mr Radinski ... good ... Now indicate to the right ... yes it's that little stick thing ... yes, you do pull it downwards ... yes, Mr Radinski, a little bit like that, but you didn't need to use quite so much force really ... yes, I'm sure we can get a new one. Now then, put your foot on the clutch ... good ... and put the engine into first gear ... good. Now press down on the accelerator ... no, you don't have to exaggerate ... that's better. Release the handbrake ... a bit more ... good, very good ... Accelerator ... check the rear-view mirror ... good ... accelerator ... accelerator, Mr Radinski, accelerator. Come on ... yes, that's better now. Er, clutch ... second gear ... foot off the clutch and accelerate ... oh good, Mr Radinski, very good, very good indeed. Now speed up a bit ... Er, you see that woman crossing the road ... Mr Radinski, that woman? Crossing the road? Mr Radinski? I think you should stop. Mr Radinski, stop ... stop ... STOP!

Yes, Mr Radinski, it is a good thing she jumped out of the way ... Concentrate on the road, please ... good ... Now as you can see, we are coming to a roundabout so we'll need to slow down and that means putting your foot on the brake and the clutch. OK? ... Brake and clutch ... Mr Radinski? ... Mr Radinski? ... There's a lorry on the roundabout ... right in front of us ... not the accelerator, Mr Radinski, the brake ... the brake, Mr Radinski ... the brake ... the clutch ... the brake! The brake! ... The brake ...

Yes, yes, Mr Radinski ... the truck driver was very rude ... Yes, I agree, he used some very bad words ... Yes, it was very unkind of him to suggest that you needed your head examining ... Yes, I'm sure he would have been more sympathetic if he had remembered what it was like to learn to drive ... Yes, you're right, we can always get a new car ... Yes, Mr Radinski, I think we are going to have to walk home ... Yes, yes, Mr Radinski. That is the end of this lesson.

Track 16

CHRIS: You can't beat a place with lovely home-cooked food and friendly service. I go to a place like that everyday – sometimes I just have a cup of tea and a cake and often have my lunch here. A fresh sandwich or a piece of home-made pie and some chips. They all know me there and they know how I like things – they really make me feel at home. I like that. I don't have to dress up – that's not really my cup of tea I go there in my work clothes – it's cheap too.

JED: For me the best way to eat is – you get in, get served quickly, get out and get on with your life. No sitting around waiting while they bring you your food, no worrying about whether you'll like it or not. I like places where I know everything on the menu and how it tastes, so there are no surprises. Where everything's clean and hygienic and the service is first class – polite professionals who say 'please' and 'thank you' and don't expect a tip. The food's not delicious, but it's good, it fills you up and it's great value.

JULIA: I love the whole restaurant-going experience. I love to make a reservation, get dressed up to go, make a real occasion of it. I read magazines and look for recommendations for new restaurants in the area that have great food and service and are a little luxurious and then my husband and I go there for a special treat. I think eating should be a delight, not just something you do to stay alive. I love trying new and interesting foods from all around the world and I don't mind paying for good food and delightful surroundings.

MARTIN: A restaurant is a great place to take someone on a date. I always pick a cool romantic place with soft lighting, small intimate tables, good wine and good food. The music should be not too loud, so that you can talk to the person you're with and really get to know her. Finding the right type of place can be crucial – it has to be just right to create the right atmosphere. You need your date's attention to be on you, not on the people around you or the music.

NAOMI: I love these self-service places where you can eat as much as you want. I have a pretty large, healthy appetite and I'm a student and restaurants are normally so expensive. I never get enough food in a fancy restaurant, anyway. I like big places with lots of variety where you can help yourself to the food that you want and it's all included in one price. That way I don't have to feel guilty about how much I'm spending – I'm actually saving money by eating more! I don't care if there's no imported caviar, I like plain food, that's not spicy, but nice and fresh.

Track 17

I never felt magic crazy as this
I never saw moons knew the meaning of the sea
I never held emotion in the palm of my hand
Or felt sweet breezes in the top of a tree
But now you're here
Brighten my northern sky.

I've been a long time that I'm waiting
Been a long timethat I'm blown
I've been a long time that I've wandered
Through the people I have known
Oh, if you would and you could
Straighten my new mind's eye.

Would you love me for my money
Would you love me for my head
Would you love me through the winter
Would you love me 'til I'm dead
Oh, if you would and you could
Come blow your horn on high.

I never felt magic crazy as this
I never saw moons knew the meaning of the sea
I never held emotion in the palm of my hand
Or felt sweet breezes in the top of a tree
But now you're here
Brighten my northern sky.

Track 18

PRESENTER: Diana is from Hyderabad in Southern India. Her parents split up when she was 13 and from the age of 14 she moved around, taking various jobs, and at the age of 18, she went to try and find work in Mumbai, then called Bombay.

DIANA: I had 250 rupees in my pocket. Now 250 rupees is the equivalent of about umm four pounds, and the person who was a family friend who was supposed to meet me at the station wasn't there, and then I went knocking from one door to the other looking for accommodation and umm it's a very bizarre story but I did get accommodation. Someone sent me to somebody else and they said – like you call them 'bedsits' here, in India you call them paying guests and they said 'oh so-and-so person keeps paying guests go there', and I got sent from one place to the other off this main road and umm I knocked on this lady's door and my watch said 7.30 and she opened the door and I said 'look someone told me – can't remember where down the line – someone said you keep, you know, paying guests,' and she said 'no I don't, not any more, I've stopped for the last three years,' and then I heard the English news in the background. Now the English news is from 9.30 to 9.45 and I said 'Is that the English news?' She said 'Yes, and what is a young girl like you doing on your own on the streets at this time?' and I said 'but it can't be because the English news is at 9.30'. She said, 'Yes, a quarter to ten,' and I showed her my watch and it stopped at 7.30 and she said, 'Come inside.' She was a Pakistani woman. She was married to an Englishman. She said, 'Come inside.' She says, 'my hair's standing and I just think God has sent you to me,' and she took me in. She said, 'Bring all your stuff and come tomorrow and umm go and get a job. When you get a job, then you can start paying me.' So that's the ... it's it's just everything. I believe that everything you try to do, if you put yourself out there and give it your all ... you will ... you will achieve it. I think it's very important that you look back and you connect with those experiences and you remember them as clearly as yesterday because if not, the superficial nonsense that goes on in your life like today can very easily take over you and you can lose perspective.

Track 19

DIANA: ... I think it's very important that you look back and you connect with those experiences and you remember them as clearly as yesterday because if not, the superficial nonsense that goes on in your life like today can very easily take over you and you can lose perspective.

PRESENTER: But Diana didn't lose perspective. After a succession of jobs – including managing two of India's most famous pop stars – she was entered into the Miss India beauty competition and she won it. Next she found herself representing her country in the Miss World competition, something that must have been quite daunting for the 23-year-old.

DIANA: Your biggest fear is 'I shouldn't trip' and because you've got these really high heels and these long long gowns and you've got all these steps that you're walking up and down and it's live on television you've got ... thousands of people watching ...

INTERVIEWER: watched by ...

DIANA: ... by millions. It is huge. Everybody watches it. You have more people watching them in India than you'd have them watching the Wimbledon finals or something, you know, or the Olympic Games or something. Yeah. Umm and your biggest fear is 'I should not go blank' because you're asked questions on stage and yeah, you can just freeze.

PRESENTER: But Diana didn't freeze. In front of a huge worldwide audience she heard a voice announce that Miss India, Diana Hayden, was the new Miss World.

DIANA: Oooh you feel numb. The ... you know it's it's a saturation point. It's too much for you to digest that your grin is stuck on your face. It was stuck on my face for weeks. I would position that crown in such a way that as soon as I opened my eyes I would see my crown. I did that for weeks. Ha ha. It was such a great feeling. You just you're just grinning and you are just numb. If that's what euphoria is, you know, umm you you can't speak very clearly. You speak but you're just so excited you're tripping over your own words, and immediately there was a press conference on stage itself and it's like ooh ooh ooh because you go from being nobody, a regular person. That's not fair. It's not a nobody. You go from being a regular person to being in every newspaper around the world and everyone knows. It went from going in a bus with 87 other girls to 'and Miss World 1997 is Miss India' to a stretch limousine, with bodyguards, where the heads of the company moved out of the presidential suite and I took over and chaperones and that's what it was right since then. You sit in the cockpits for take-offs and landings. You get treated like a queen you, you know, you have private planes, and all these flights and umm the red carpet and it's just Lights! Camera! Action!

Track 20

MARCUS: Are you ready to do your duty for Rome?
COMMODUS [1]: Yes, Father.
MARCUS: You will not be emperor.
COMMODUS [2]: Which wiser, older man is to take my place?
MARCUS: My powers will pass to Maximus to hold in trust until the Senate is ready to rule once more. Rome is to be a Republic again.
COMMODUS: Maximus? [3]
MARCUS: My decision disappoints you?
COMMODUS: You wrote to me once, listing the four chief virtues – wisdom, justice, fortitude and temperance. As I read the list, I knew I had none of them. But I have other virtues, Father – ambition, that can be a virtue when it drives us to excel; resourcefulness; courage, perhaps not on the battlefield but there are many forms of courage; devotion, to my family, to you. But none of my virtues were on your list. Even then, it was as if you didn't want me for your son.
MARCUS [4]: Oh, Commodus, you go too far.
COMMODUS [5]: I searched the faces of the gods for ways to please you, to make you proud ... One kind word, one full hug while you pressed me to your chest and held me tight, would have been like the sun on my heart for a thousand years ... What is it in me you hate so much? All I ever wanted was to live up to you, Caesar, Father.
MARCUS: Commodus, (deep breath); your faults as a son, is my failure as a father.
COMMODUS: Father, I would butcher the whole world if you would only love me! [9] (crying)

Track 21

PRESENTER: Today's book extract comes from *White Teeth*, a novel by Zadie Smith.
Archie Jones, a British man, and Samad Iqbal, originally from Bangladesh, have been friends since they were soldiers together in the British Army in World War II. They both live and work in London where Archie is married to a Jamaican woman named Clara with whom he has one nine-year-old daughter, Irie, and Samad is married to Alsana and has twin boys, Millat and Magid, who are also nine. Samad, who works as a waiter, has decided that Britain in 1984 is an unhealthy place to bring up his sons, and is planning to send Magid to Samad's family in Bangladesh in order to offer him a better education and upbringing. He has not told anyone except Archie about his

plan; Magid does not know that his father is going to send him away. Archie has agreed to drive Samad and the child to the airport so that Magid can be put on the plane at 3 am.
READER: Samad arrives, clasps Archie's right hand in his own and feels the coldness of his friend's fingers, feels the great debt he owes him. Involuntarily, he blows a cloud of frozen breath into his face. 'I won't forget this, Archibald,' he is saying, 'I won't forget what you do for me tonight, my friend.'
Archie shuffles about awkwardly. 'Sam, before you – there's something I have to ...'
But Samad is already reaching for the door, and Archie's explanation must follow the sight of three shivering children in the back seat like a limp punch-line.
'They *woke up*, Sam. They were all sleeping in the same room – a sleepover, like. Nothing I could do. I just put coats over their pyjamas – I couldn't risk Clara hearing – I *had* to bring them.'
Irie asleep; curled up with her head on the ashtray and her feet resting on the gearbox, but Millat and Magid reaching out for their father gleefully, pulling at his flares, chucking him on the chin.
'Hey, Abba! Where we going, Abba? To a secret disco party? Are we really?'
Samad looks severely at Archie; Archie shrugs.
'We're going on a trip to an airport. To Heathrow.'
'Wow!'
'And then when we get there, Magid ... Magid ...'
It is like a dream. Samad feels the tears before he can stop them; he reaches out to his eldest-son-by-two-minutes and holds him so tight to his chest that he snaps the arm of his glasses. 'And then Magid is going on a trip with Auntie Zinat.'
'Will he come back?' It is Millat. 'It would be cool if he didn't come back!'
Magid prises himself from his father's headlock. 'Is it far? Will I be back in time for Monday – only I've got to see how my photosynthesis is for science. I took two plants: put one in the cupboard and one in the sunlight – and I've got to see, Abba, *I've got to see which one ...*'
Years from now, even hours after that plane leaves, this will be history that Samad tries *not* to remember. That his memory makes no effort to retain. A sudden stone submerged. False teeth floating silently to the bottom of the glass.
'Will I get back for school, Abba?'
'Come on,' says Archie, solemnly from the front seat. 'We've got to get cracking if we're going to make it.'
'You'll be in a school on Monday, Magid. I promise. Now sit back in your seats, go on. For Abba, please.'

Track 22

Story 1

And finally on the news tonight, in Providence, Rhode Island, an armoured car driver was robbed of four money sacks today. But what the robber didn't know was that instead of bundles of banknotes each bag contained only 80 dollars in pennies. Try as he might, the thief, weighed down with coins, could not make a fast getaway. Police easily caught the man, David Posman, 33, as he tried to run away with the bags which weighed 30 pounds each.

Story 2

In London today a very unusual story of the perfect crime that went wrong, the bank robbery that failed. Everything seemed to be just right: the timing had been planned to the minute, the escape route was ready, even the hiding place for the money had been carefully prepared. The getaway driver had been handpicked as someone who could be trusted. The robbery went without a hitch and the robber ran out of the bank with over £100,000 in cash. Unfortunately for the robber, Wayne Smith from East

London, when he reached the getaway car, his friend the driver, wanting to make the escape as fast as possible, ran him over. Smith and his accomplice are both in hospital tonight where they are reported to be in a stable condition.

Story 3

Some news from San Antonio that shows you you have to be careful what you ask for. Brian Tilbury was convicted of burglary after entering a home and stealing a TV and stereo last month. In court today, the judge sentenced Tilbury to seven years in prison. According to witnesses at the court, this appeared to upset Tilbury and he proceeded to beg the judge not to sentence him to seven years as seven was his unlucky number. The judge heard his request and agreed to help the man. He sentenced him to eight years. Tilbury's lawyers have vowed to appeal the decision.

Story 4

Some crime news from across the Atlantic. In Florida today, Reinero Torres Jr was finally prosecuted after going to court for a third time. The first two times he had been found not guilty of the charges of shoplifting from a local store and had gone free. Today he was finally convicted at the third attempt. His crime? Stealing law books from the court house library which he was using to prepare the defence for his first two cases.

Story 5

And finally on the news tonight, a story that shows that crime really doesn't pay. A man was arrested tonight after he attempted to hold up a grocery store. It seems the criminal came into the grocery store wearing a paper bag over his head with two eyeholes cut out so that he could see. In the course of the robbery, the eyeholes shifted and he found that he was no longer able to see what he was doing – or what anyone else was doing. When the robber tried to move the bag back so he could continue with the robbery, the bag opened completely and the sales clerk was able to see the man's face. The clerk recognized him as a regular customer and called the police immediately after the thief made his getaway, without taking anything. The man was arrested soon after and will appear in court next week charged with attempted robbery.

That's all we have time for this evening, but we'll be back at 10 o'clock with a local news update.

Track 23

PRESENTER: Jan Blake is a storyteller. Not just the kind of person who comes into work or school and tells you what happened to them the night before, but a professional storyteller who stands up in front of large audiences of children and adults and tells traditional stories, some from her own Jamaican background, some from Britain where she was born and brought up, and others from around the world. She *performs* stories, and gets audiences to participate by shouting out, clapping and responding.

JAN: What are stories for? I think, I think stories ... this is my personal opinion, this isn't ... er ... a kind of tried and tested theory, but my personal opinion is that when someone tells a story in that arena, at the moment that the story is being told everything about being human is accepted, yeah? The good, the bad. Every single experience of being human is in that room with everybody and it's almost, there's no judgement of what it means to be a human being in that moment. Does that make sense? So, what the audience gets from it I think is tha- a mirror is held up and I say to the audience this is us, aren't we great? Or aren't we stupid, or aren't we fascinating or aren't we vengeful or aren't we wonderful lovers or aren't we ... this is the whole gamut of human experience can be found in a story I think, and I think that there's something very

fundamental that I can't put my finger on and say what it is. But it happens when stories are told, the visualising of the story, the sound of the storyteller's voice, the contact with the audience, the er asides if you like, the recognition of the human condition – all of those things are in the room with you when you tell a story, when you hear a story, and I think that's what the audience gets out of it umm, the opportunity to delve deep into your own consciousness, your own subconscious, your own imagination and experience something universal. I think that's what happens when you hear a story, that's what happens when I tell a story.

Track 24

PRESENTER: Jan, who was born and brought up in Manchester in the United Kingdom, didn't start as a storyteller. At the age of 19, she joined a travelling theatre group. And it was when she was working in a show in London some years later that she met the Ghanaian actress Eno Sourcey who suggested that she should audition for a storytelling group called '*Common Law*'.

JAN: And I said oh where where can you earn some decent money then, and she said oh as a storyteller so I said what's that? And she said oh I'm a storyteller, I think you'd be really good, I think you should come along to '*Common Law*' and you should audition. You have to bring a story from your own tradition, a game from your own tradition and a song from your own tradition. So my mum had sung me songs and taught me games when I was a child so I had that. I had to go and find a story. I didn't have any stories that ... on hand, so I went and bought a book by Philip Sherlock, *West Indian Folk Tales*, and I, I found a story called *Why Cat and Dog are no longer friends* and I read that and read it and read it and read it and read it and I haven't told that story since, I have to s- I haven't told that story for 20 years. It would be interesting to tell it again now after all this time but I read it and read it and read it and I knew that I couldn't learn the whole story word for word, there was no way it was going to be possible, so I just had to simply tell it. So I went along to this space in Brixton umm and met the rest of '*Common Law*' and they said, OK, can you tell us your story? And I sat there and I opened my mouth and out came this story and I was really surprised because I'd I'd never told it to anybody. It just came out and it worked and I could see on their faces that it was working for them as well as was working for me and from that moment I haven't looked back. I have not wanted to do any, anything else but tell stories since that moment.

Track 25

PRESENTER: Jan Blake's storytelling performances are electrifying. The Swedish story expert Eulf Ardstrom calls her the 'British-Jamaican storytelling volcano'. Sometimes, though, she finds herself in awkward situations, like the time a couple of years ago, when she was booked to appear at the Spitalfields Theatre in London – often called 'The Spitz'.

JAN: Ah ... I work sometimes with a percussionist called Crispin Robinson and he's notoriously late and the person who had booked the session was late and I was at the at the Spitz on my own and Crispin turned up five minutes before we were supposed to go on and two of the stories he'd never heard me tell before, so he had to play to these two stories, and one of the stories had a song in that needed harmonies and he had to sing them because the story had to work with these, and I, I'm very demanding like that I think. Umm, the fact is that when I work with Crispin I can do that. So five minutes before, he turned up and he was like 'Oh God my brain and the traffic's awful and just let me lie here for five minutes,' and I said 'we're on in five minutes' and he said 'er yeah just give me five minutes,' so as he lay on the ground I just said 'OK, if you ... there's two of the stories you haven't heard. This is one of them, it's about a hunter, this happens,' and and I kind of went through the sequence of events, and I said, 'we're gonna need dramatic drumming here, we're gonna need running drumming here, we're gonna need, you know, a kind of a lyrical moving here, that's that's what we're gonna need. And then the other story is a Jamaican story umm this this is the song.' I sang it to him and I said, 'give me some harmonies', he gave me the harmonies straight away and then boom we had to go on and do the story and it was the best storytelling exp – cos we were on the edge of our creativity, risk, yeah, we couldn't fail. It was one of those situations where we, I was not going to let us fail regardless of the circumstances around it, that was all these people, the place was humming with people, it was packed and that also, all these people in the audience all came to hear Jan Blake and Crispin Robinson so they were willing it to be a fantastic experience and then there's a song that I always start with and I asked the audience to join in and sing it and they weren't giving us themselves and I said to them 'Look you know, he was late, he was late you know, I'm slightly, you know, off kilter and we are here together and this has to work for all of us... and so we worked, sang the song, all, the harmonies were fantastic, the storytelling was great and it's the first time I've experienced storytelling where it's as though we're not actually in the room, you know, we left the room and we were in a different space altogether, all of us were in a completely different space together and umm it was a fantastic experience, fantastic.

Track 26

You're listening to the self-guided tour of the Van Gogh Museum in Amsterdam.

Vincent Willem van Gogh was born March 30th, 1853, in Groot-Zundert, son of a Dutch Protestant pastor. He was a moody young man who was easily bored and by the age of 27 he had been in turn a salesman in an art gallery, a French tutor, a theological student and an evangelist in Belgium.

In 1886, Van Gogh went to Paris to live with his brother Theo van Gogh, an art dealer, and became familiar with the new art movements developing at the time. Here, Van Gogh began to experiment with the modern techniques that were popular at the time.

In 1888, Van Gogh left Paris for southern France, where he painted scenes of the fields, the peasants and lives typical of the people who lived in the countryside. During this period, living at Arles, he began to use the swirling brush strokes and intense yellows, greens and blues associated with some of his most famous paintings such as *Bedroom at Arles*, and *Starry Night*.

In his enthusiasm, he persuaded the painter Paul Gauguin, whom he had met earlier in Paris, to join him. After less than two months, they began to have violent disagreements, culminating in a quarrel in which Van Gogh wildly threatened Gauguin with a razor. That same night, in a fit of deep remorse brought on by his many mental problems, Van Gogh cut off part of his own ear.

For a time, he was in a hospital at Arles. He then spent a year in the nearby mental asylum of Saint-Rémy, working between repeated spells of madness. Finally he left the mental asylum and lived for three months in a town called Auvers. Just after completing one of his most remarkable paintings, the ominous *Crows in the Wheatfields*, he shot himself on July 27th, 1890, and died two days later.

During his life, Van Gogh wrote more than 700 letters to his brother Theo, and these letters give us a remarkable picture of how he approached his art, what he painted and when, and his state of mind. He left behind about 750 paintings and 160 drawings. He only ever sold one painting in his lifetime, but now his most famous works (such as *Sunflowers*) sell for millions of dollars.

Press the number on the wall to hear about the works that you now see in front of you.

Track 27

You're listening to the self-guided tour of the Van Gogh Museum in Amsterdam. These exhibits are numbers 27 and 28.

The two pictures you see before you were both painted when Van Gogh was in Paris from 1886 to 1888. In that two-year period, he painted 27 self-portraits. This was because he often could not afford models and so painted himself in order to experiment with colour and different techniques.

The first picture, number 27, shows Vincent in an elegant suit and hat. It seems that Vincent used this picture in order to study grey. The picture is full of varying tones of grey and even the eyes, which are normally green, are painted in a dramatic blue-grey tone. The hat is made of felt. The red in his face and particularly in the beard makes the head stand out from the background. The kind of clothes he is wearing suggest fashionable Paris at that time and it seems that he is also advertising himself as a portrait painter. Van Gogh was always looking for customers for portraits as an important source of income.

The second picture, number 28, shows Van Gogh doing a study of colour yet again. Here, he seems to be looking at the effect of yellow against a blue background. Note also the range of colours in the jacket, bow-tie and background. The straw hat seems a strange combination with the suit that he's wearing, and this makes it clear that the purpose of the picture was to experiment with colour.

Please press 29 to hear about the next painting or 0 to hear more information on the life of Vincent van Gogh.

Track 28

Small Boy by Norman MacCraig
Small Boy
He picked up a pebble
and threw it in the sea.

And another, and another.
He couldn't stop.

He wasn't trying to fill the sea.
He wasn't trying to empty the beach.

He was just throwing away,
nothing else but.

Like a kitten playing
he was practising for the future

when there'll be so many things
he'll want to throw away

if only his fingers will unclench
and let them go.

Track 29

An extract from *Space Station 5*
They had been up here for five years. Five years for five people, cut off from earth since World War IV. True, the Moonshuttle came every six months with a supply of food, but it was pilotless. They had not been able to make contact with Moonbase for two years. Cathy said it was weird.

'You say that three times a day,' Rosie answered.

'Well it's true. It's weird and I don't think I can stand it much longer.'

'Oh for Jupiter's sake shut up! Go and play eight-dimensional death-chess and leave me alone. You drive me crazy!'

'You shouldn't have spoken to me like that,' Cathy said quietly and left the cabin. The door hissed behind her.

Track 30

NEWSREADER: In London today a very unusual story of the perfect crime that went wrong, the bank robbery that failed. Everything seemed to be just right: the timing had been planned to the minute, the escape route was ready, even the hiding place for the money had been carefully prepared. The getaway driver had been handpicked as someone who could be trusted. The robbery went without a hitch and the robber ran out of the bank with over £100,000 in cash. Unfortunately for the robber, Wayne Smith from East London, when he reached the getaway car, his friend the driver, wanting to make the escape as fast as possible, ran him over. Smith and his accomplice are both in hospital tonight where they are reported to be in a stable condition.

Track 31

NEWSREADER: Some crime news from across the Atlantic. In Florida today, Reinero Torres Jr was finally prosecuted after going to court for a third time. The first two times, he had been found not guilty of the charges of shoplifting from a local store and had gone free. Today he was finally convicted at the third attempt. His crime? Stealing law books from the court house library which he was using to prepare the defence for his first two cases.

Track 32

Carmen

HUSBAND: She spends all her time potholing.

Beep

HUSBAND: Yes. I call it crawling through underground caves on your hands and knees.

Beep

HUSBAND: Well I think it is and I've begged her to stop but she says she can't. She's obsessed by it and that's the truth.

CARMEN: It's not that dangerous.

Beep

CARMEN: Well yes, but I've been potholing for ten years now and I've never had any trouble.

Marcus

MARCUS: Yes, it's true, I do like playing golf very much.

Beep

MARCUS: Oh no, I'm not addicted to it or anything. It's something I do just for fun.

Beep

MARCUS: Two weeks? You can't be serious.

Beep

MARCUS: Not a long time? You're joking. I begin to feel really unhappy if I don't have a round of golf about twice a week. Oh dear. I suppose that means I am a bit of an addict, doesn't it!

Track 33

1

Jack

JACK: People call us nerds in anoraks, I know, but we aren't doing anybody any harm.

INTERVIEWER: Well no.

Beep

INTERVIEWER: You do?

Beep

INTERVIEWER: I'll take your word for it.

Beep

INTERVIEWER: Yes, I imagine they are.

2

Ellie

INTERVIEWER: Isn't what you do really dangerous?

Beep

INTERVIEWER: But don't you ever get scared? I know I would be.

Beep

INTERVIEWER: I don't think I'd be very keen.

Track 34

WOMAN: Do you believe in the paranormal, you know, fortune-telling, astrology, past lives, etc.?

a *Beep*

WOMAN: Who's he?

b *Beep*

WOMAN: So you don't believe in that stuff now?

c *Beep*

WOMAN: Oh come on, you're not saying all that is complete rubbish?

d *Beep*

WOMAN: Well yes, I read my stars all the time.

e *Beep*

WOMAN: Fine. That describes me perfectly.

Track 35

1 *Beep*

MAN: Well there's an explanation.

2 *Beep*

MAN: I don't know. But there's always an explanation. There isn't any mystery out there.

3 *Beep*

MAN: Not exactly. They're not lying, no. They're often trying to make sense of a chaotic confusing world. And we're all susceptible to suggestion.

4 *Beep*

MAN: Well suppose you saw a headline saying 'Baby is a space alien'. You wouldn't believe it, would you?

5 *Beep*

MAN: But suppose you kept seeing it in different papers, heard it on shows, heard it from the mouths of people you trusted. You'd believe it then, perhaps?

6 *Beep*

MAN: Well there you are.

7 *Beep*

MAN: No. What?

8 *Beep*

MAN: Why?

9 *Beep*

Track 36

CUSTOMER: Do you have frog's legs?

Beep

CUSTOMER: Do you serve lobsters here?

Beep

CUSTOMER: Hey watch out! Your thumb's in my soup!

Beep

WAITER: How did you find your steak, sir?

Beep

CUSTOMER: How long will my sausages be?

Beep

CUSTOMER: Waiter! There's a fly in my soup!

Beep

CUSTOMER: Waiter! Your tie is in my soup.
Beep
CUSTOMER: What's this fly doing in my soup?
Beep

Track 37

REPORTER: Thanks for agreeing to this interview. I'll try and be as quick as possible. So here's my first question: what makes you happy?
Beep
REPORTER: How do you relax?
Beep
REPORTER: What three words best describe you?
Beep
REPORTER: When you were a child, what was your favourite food?
Beep
REPORTER: What is your most vivid childhood memory?
Beep
REPORTER: What words or phrases in English do you use most often?
Beep
REPORTER: Which living person would you most like to meet?
Beep
REPORTER: What is the most important lesson life has taught you?
Beep
REPORTER: Thanks very much. I think I've got enough there. Thanks very much for your time.
Beep

Track 38

INTERVIEWER 1: Good morning. Come in and sit down.
Beep
INTERVIEWER 1: Now then, I wonder if you could tell us why you are interested in this job.
Beep
INTERVIEWER 1: Thank you for that answer. What qualities do you think someone would need for this job?
Beep
INTERVIEWER 1: I see. Do you think you have these qualities?
Beep
INTERVIEWER 2: Moving on, I'd like to ask you to give us some idea about yourself. Do you have any hobbies, for example?
Beep

INTERVIEWER 2: I see, and what is your favourite way of relaxing?
Beep
INTERVIEWER 1: We've come to the moment in the interview when you can ask us any questions you might have. Do you have any questions?
Beep
INTERVIEWER 1: Well that just about finishes this interview for the moment. Thank you very much. If you want to wait in the library we'll let you know if we need you again. Could you send the next person in?
Beep
INTERVIEWER 1: Not at all. It was a pleasure meeting you. Goodbye.

Track 39

QUESTIONER: Could you list your six items of furniture and say why you have chosen them?
Beep
QUESTIONER: Thanks. Those are interesting choices. Now what about colours? What colour have you chosen for the carpet?
Beep
QUESTIONER: Any special reason for that?
Beep
QUESTIONER: And what about the walls and the ceiling?
Beep
QUESTIONER: Well that's all very interesting. Now I wonder if you could say in your own words what kind of 'feel' you want the room to have. How would you describe it?
Beep
QUESTIONER: Thanks very much for that. Goodbye.

ANSWER KEY

PART A: LISTENING

Listening 1

1
The answer is d.

2
a $100
b markets
c the local store
d once
e $500
f a couple of CDs
g once every two weeks
h school cafeteria

3
a spendthrift
b major
c dilemma
d budget
e expenditure
f cut down
g groceries
h varies
i specials
j roommates

4
a spendthrift = someone who spends money carelessly
b major = student
c dilemma = difficult problem
d budget = plan of what you earn and what you save
e expenditure = what you spend
f cut down = reduce
g groceries = food
h varies = changes
i specials = reduced offers
j roommates = friends who share a flat

5
prudent, down-to-earth

Listening 2

1
The answer is b.

2
a £20
b £2

3
a F
b T
c T
d T
e T
f T
g T
h T
i F

4
a shut up
b make matters worse
c get the message
d couldn't care less
e comes to the conclusion
f all keen
g a piece of cake
h weeping
i flabbergasted
j put me out of my misery

5
1 c
2 f
3 e
4 j
5 i
6 a
7 d
8 h
9 g
10 b

6
C is probably the best answer.

Listening 3

1
Peter   b
Jane   c
Kate   a
Betty   d
Peter is middle-aged (he talks about having a box camera as a child).
Jane and Kate are young women (Kate lived in Thailand with her parents ten years earlier).
Betty is an elderly woman (she makes her childhood sound distant).

2
a Peter
b Peter
c Kate
d Kate
e Jane
f Jane
g Kate
h Betty
i Peter
j Jane
k Kate (and her family)

3
a Bangkok
b The Grand Palace
c Thailand
d Arosa
e Machu Picchu
f The Grand Palace
g Machu Picchu
h Cuzco
i Arosa
j Sally
k Cuzco

4
a 10
b 8
c 5
d 6
e 7
f 2
g 12
h 11
i 9
j 4
k 3
l 1

Listening 4

1
The correct answer is d.

2
a 2
b 2
c 1
d both
e both
f both
g 2
h both
i 2
j both
k both

3
a 9
b 4
c 5
d 8
e 3
f 6
g 7
h 2
i 1

4
The statement is false. Hag thinks that people will still pay for a hand-made print that's printed from each element.

5

a darkroom
b whole
c candlelight
d naked
e flame
f flame
g light-bulb
h digital
i computer
j printed
k reproduction
l digital

Listening 5

1

The extract comes from *Little House on the Prairie*.

2

a the moonlight
b her father holding a gun
c a wolf's howl
d her father and Jack
e knowing the wolves couldn't get in

3

a a bed covering; two
b a dog
c because there's no glass in them
d Laura's sister

4

a growled and showed
b she knew better than
c lifted her up
d folded her arms
e moved back a little
f take care of you all
g on the other side of

Listening 6

1

Danny: fishing / angling
Carmen: potholing
Jack: train-spotting
Marcus: golf
Ellie: skydiving

2

a Danny
b Carmen's husband
c Carmen's husband
d Carmen
e Jack's interviewer
f Jack
g Marcus
h Marcus
i Ellie
j Jack

3

1 I've begged. (b)
2 I'm not addicted to it. (g)
3 I'll take your word for it.(e)
4 It's not for everybody. (i)
5 Nerds in anoraks. (j)
6 The only downside. (f)
7 You can't be serious. (h)

4

a I call it crawling through underground caves on your hands and knees.
b It's just that feeling of surfing the sky, plunging through the air.
c Oh dear. I suppose that means I'm a bit of an addict, doesn't it!
d Oh no, I'm not addicted to it or anything. It's something I do just for fun.
e People call us nerds in anoraks, I know, but we aren't doing anybody any harm.
f Sometimes, a little, but you get that rush of adrenaline. It's just wonderful.
g That's why I like it. It gives you time to think.
h The only downside is that it can be pretty cold just standing on a station platform all day.
i Well, yes, but I've been potholing for ten years now and I've never had any trouble.
j Yeah, I'm an angler. Like my Dad.

Listening 7

1

The activities which are mentioned are: ice-skating, tennis, swimming, aerobics, ballet and judo.

2

a 2
b 1
c 2
d 1
e 3
f 3
g 3
h 2

3

a 5
b 11
c 9
d 10
e 2
f X (no match)
g 6
h 4
i 1
j 3

k 7
l 8

4

a 6
b 1
c 8
d 7
e 3
f 4
g 2
h 5

5

a consult
b take advantage of
c concludes
d court
e accompanied by
f leisure
g facilities
h matches

Listening 8

2

The correct order is **g, f, d, e, b, h, a, c.**

3

Albert: frightened, fur coat, noise, phobia, rabbit
Behaviourism:1900–1950, habit formation, influential, prize
Pavlov: bell, dogs, food, Russia
Rats: bar, light

4

a Habit formation is training people or animals to do something through repeated controlled practice tied to stimulus-response and rewards.
b They thought they were going to be fed.
c They learnt to press a bar when a light went on.
d He was a young boy who had a pet rabbit.
e Because the scientists made a loud and frightening noise every time he was near his rabbit.
f He became frightened of them too – because of the experiment.
g They were not keen on the idea.

5

a this
b give
c correctly
d then
e once
f way
g necessary
h theory
i depends
j habituated

k thinking
l type
m example
n meant
o result
p even
q food
r rats
s had
t when
u food
v end
w light

Listening 9

1
The activities connected with the future are:
a astrology
b ESP
d fortune-telling
g palmistry
h tarot cards

2
a sceptic
b believer

3
a 6
b 3
c 5
d 2
e 7
f 1
g 4

4
a pizza
b restaurant
c paranormal
d saying
e began / started
f incident
g could
h knowing
i rational
j believe
k cynical / sceptical
l fun
m answer

5
a It's all made up.
b It's all made up.
c It's all junk.
d There's an explanation.
e They're not lying, but they're trying to make sense of a chaotic, confusing world.
f We're all susceptible to suggestion.

6
a don't believe in
b complete rubbish
c How am I
d out there
e that one out
f would you
g where's the fun
h depends

Listening 10

1
a 5
b 3
c 7
d 8
e 1
f 4
g 2
h 6

2
a F
b T
c F
d F
e T
f T
g F

3

4
1
a Yes, I have.
b Yes, on my father's farm.
c I crashed into the gate and the car had to be repaired.
d I drove into a wall and now the radiator needs replacing.
2
a He used some very bad words.
b He said I needed my head examining. That was very unkind.
c If he had remembered what it was like to learn to drive he would have been more sympathetic.
d You can always get a new car.
e Are we going to have to walk home?
f Is that the end of the lesson?

5
a 8
b 6
c 2, 3, 4
d 7
e 1
f 5
g 5
h 2, 3, 4
i 9
The verbs *select*, *switch off* and *turn*, and the noun *steering-wheel* are not in the recording.

Listening 11

1
a Jed
b Naomi
c Julia
d Chris
e Martin

2
a Chris, Jed, Naomi
b Jed
c Chris
d Naomi
e Jed
f Julia
g Chris
h Martin
i Julia
j Jed
k Martin
l Chris

3
a M
b Je
c Ju
d C
e N
f Ju
g N
h Je
i C
j M

4
Chris

Food	home-cooked
Service	friendly
Atmosphere	feels at home
Price	cheap

Jed

Food	not delicious
Service	polite, fast, first class
Atmosphere	no surprises; clean, hygienic
Price	great value

Julia

Food	great food
Service	great service
Atmosphere	luxurious, delightful surroundings
Price	not important (probably expensive)

Martin

Food	good
Atmosphere	romantic, soft lighting, small intimate tables, no loud music

Naomi

Food	plenty of it, variety, plain, fresh
Service	self-service
Atmosphere	simple
Price	cheap – eat what you want for one set price

Listening 12

1

a pick, go with
b absolutely
c When all is said and done
d delicate
e first rate

3

1 e
2 b
3 a
4 h
5 d
6 g
7 c
8 i
9 f
10 e
11 b
12 a

4

a my, high, eye
b sweet, breezes, been, people, meaning, sea, me
c known
d dead
e straighten, waiting

Listening 13

2

a Hyderabad, in India.
b Her parents split up.
c She went from door to door asking to rent a room.
d Half past seven.
e Because she realised the poor young girl didn't even have a watch that worked and she took pity on her.
f You will succeed if you try. You have to remember moments like that.

3

She won Miss World in 1997.

4

a She was afraid of tripping on her high heels.
b Millions.
c Numb.
d She looked at it as soon as she woke up.
e She couldn't stop grinning.

5

a A sitting room and bedroom combined which you can rent.
b We're scared or shocked. Diana reports the Pakistani woman as saying 'my hair's standing' which may well be a Pakistani English way of saying the same thing.
c A lot of effort.
d No. You can't think at all.
e Fantastically happy.
f To stumble over your words, to mix them up as you speak.
g Ordinary.
h Keep a watch on someone (and look after them) to make sure they behave appropriately.
i The place at the front of an aeroplane where a pilot sits.

6

a numb
b too
c grin
d stuck
e position
f soon
g see
h weeks

i grinning
j euphoria
k clearly
l conference
m like
n being
o fair
p newspaper
q knows

Listening 14

1

a Maximus
b Commodus and Maximus
c Marcus

2

a That he will not be the next emperor.
b Maximus.
c He wants Rome to be a republic – that is without an emperor or a monarch.

d He didn't want him as his son.
e A kind word or a hug.
f Marcus says that he himself has failed as a father.
g His father to love him.

3

a 1
b 10
c 2
d 7
e 3
f 4
g 6
h 9
i 8
j 5

4

Marcus' list: wisdom, justice, fortitude and temperance
Commodus' list: ambition, resourcefulness, courage, devotion

5

a 7
b 8
c 6
d 5
e 3
f 9
g 4
h 2
i 1

Listening 15

1

a Archie and Samad
b Clara
c Archie and Clara's daughter
d Alsana
e twin sons of Samad and Alsana
f Samad
g Magid
h Archie

2

Millat and Magrid argue a lot, the way brothers do. Archie and Samed are good friends, who trust each other.

3

a Scene 25 – In the book Archie does not explain about the children until Samad has seen the children in the back of the car.

Scene 27 – Irie waking up and starting to cry.
b Archie's explanation of why he had to bring the other children, the children calling Samad 'Daddy' instead of 'Abba'.

c Archie: 'That's what friends are for, Sam, but I have to tell you something.'
Irie: 'I want to go home.'
Millat: 'Shut up about your stupid plants!'
d Samad: 'I won't forget what you do for me tonight, my friend.'
Millat: 'Will he come back? It would be cool if he didn't come back.'
Samad: 'And then when we get there, Magid … Magid …'
Archie: 'Come on. We've got to get cracking if we're going to make it.'
Samad: 'Now sit back in your seats, go on. For Abba, please.'

4
a F
b T
c T
d T
e F
f T
g F

5
a arrives
b coldness
c debt
d frozen
e reaching
f explanation
g shivering
h seat
i curled
j feet
k reaching
l pulling
m dream
n stop
o eldest
p chest
q glasses
r hours
s history
t remember
u effort
v silently

Listening 16

1
a 3
b 5
c 4
d 1
e 2

2
a Reason for arrest?
b What was stolen?
Story 1 Weight of bags stolen meant robber couldn't run.
four money sacks containing pennies

Story 2 Driver of getaway car ran robber over after he had robbed a bank.
£100,000
Story 3 Burglar had his sentence increased by the judge after complaining a seven-year sentence would bring him bad luck.
TV and stereo
Story 4 Shoplifter was caught stealing books from a library.
law books
Story 5 Robber recognised during an armed robbery.
nothing

3
a car made from strong, bullet-resistant steel
b escape
c way out
d carefully chosen
e according to plan
f found guilty of
g condemned / given a punishment
h challenge a conviction
i put on trial
j stealing from shops
k tried
l during
m moved

4
1 30-pound bags
Providence, Rhode Island
armoured car   pennies
2 injury   a lot of cash   London
3 an extra year   San Antonio
stereo
4 Florida   law books   shoplifting
5 eyeholes   grocery store   paper bag

Listening 17

1
The words that are used in Track 23 are:
a a mirror held up
b asides
d being human
g fascinating
h fundamental
i aren't we great?
m no judgement
q something universal
r stupid
s the whole gamut
t visualising
v your own subconscious

2
a She joined a travelling theatre group.
b To audition as a storyteller.
c Bring a story, a game and a song from her own tradition.

d *Why Cat and Dog are no longer friends.*
e From her mother.
f By reading and reading and reading and reading it so she could tell it her own way.
g It 'worked'; both she and the people listening liked it a lot.

3
a the Spitalfields Theatre
b Crispin Robinson
c Crispin
d Crispin
e Jan
f Jan and Crispin
g the audience
h Jan
i Jan, Crispin and the audience

4
a something that's certain to be true because people have proved it to be the case (talking about what stories are for)
b Do you understand? / Is what I am saying logical? (talking about how stories relate to human experience)
c I don't know / can't work out what it is (talking about something fundamental being found in all stories)
d to dig down (talking about listeners discovering hidden thoughts and images in themselves)
e described the events and the order they occurred in (talking of a story she had to explain to her accompanist)
f very full of people who were in an anticipatory mood (talking of her audience just before the show)
g to sing with me (talking about wanting her audience to be actively involved)
h not sure of what I'm doing / unsure of myself (talking about appearing unprepared on stage)

5
a think
b personal
c kind
d but
e that
f story
g moment
h everything
i accepted
j single
k human
l almost
m what
n being

o so
p mirror
q audience
r aren't
s fascinating
t wonderful
u human
v think
w can't

Listening 18

1

a 5
b 10
c 6
d 8
e 11
f 3
g 9
h 4
i 1
j 7
k 2

2

The picture on the left is Exhibit 28, *Man in a Straw Hat*, by Vincent van Gogh.

The picture on the right is Exhibit 27, *Man in a Felt Hat*, by Vincent van Gogh.

3

a F
b F
c T
d F
e T
f T

g F
h T
i F

4

a his moods changed
b things that were happening in the art world
c small farmers, simple country people
d circular movements with the paintbrush that show up on the canvas
e ending in / leading to
f menacing, suggesting something bad is going to happen
g different shades
h show up clearly
i pictures of people
j a tie tied in a bow at the neck

PART B: SPEAKING

Speaking 1

C

1

a

wrong o
failed a
just right oa
minute oa
ready a
money a
trusted oa
hitch o
robber o o
London o
driver oa
possible a
over oa
hospital o
condition a

D

1

[Some <u>crime</u> news] [from a<u>cross</u> the Atlantic]. [In Florida today], [Rei<u>ne</u>ro Torres Junior] [was <u>fi</u>nally prosecuted] [after going to court for a <u>third</u> time]. [The first <u>two</u> times he had been found <u>not</u> guilty] [of the charges of <u>shop</u>lifting from a local store] [and had gone <u>free</u>]. [To<u>day</u> he was <u>fi</u>nally con<u>vic</u>ted] [at the third at<u>tempt</u>]. [His <u>crime</u>?] [<u>Stealing law</u> books] [from the <u>court</u> house <u>library</u>] [which he was <u>using</u>] [to pre<u>pare</u> the defence for his <u>first</u> <u>two</u> cases.]

E

F

1

Laura scringed away from the wall. The wolf was on the other side of it. She was too scared to make a sound. The cold was not in her backbone only, it was all through her. Mary pulled the quilt over her head. Jack growled and showed his teeth at the quilt in the doorway.
'Be still, Jack,' Pa said.
Terrible howls curled all around the house, and Laura rose out of bed. She wanted to go to Pa, but she knew better than to bother him now. He turned his head and saw her standing in her nightgown.
'Want to see them?' he asked softly.
Laura couldn't say anything, but she nodded, and padded across the ground to him. He stood his gun against the wall and lifted her up to the window-hole.
There in the moonlight stood half a circle of wolves. They sat on their haunches and looked at Laura in the window, and she looked at them. She had never seen such big wolves. The biggest one was taller than Laura. He was taller even than Mary. He sat in the middle, exactly opposite Laura. Everything about him was big – his pointed ears, and pointed mouth with the tongue hanging out, and his strong shoulders and legs, and his two paws side by side, and his tail curled around the squatting haunch. His coat was shaggy grey and his eyes were glittering green.

Speaking 2

A

1

a Potholing?
b Isn't that dangerous?
c People do get trapped, though, don't they?
d So it's really important to you? You can't live without it?
e So it wouldn't matter if you didn't play for, say, two weeks?
f Why not? Two weeks isn't a very long time.

B

1

a And I get a real kick out of it.
b Yeah. It's great when you see an engine you've never seen before.
c The only downside is that it can be pretty cold just standing on a station platform all day. They're some of the windiest places on earth.
d No, not really. Not if you're careful, especially about your equipment.
e Sometimes, a little, but you get that rush of adrenaline, it's just wonderful!
f No, well it's not for everybody, obviously. But it really turns me on. It still does, even though I've been doing it for four years now. It's just that feeling of surfing the sky, plunging through the air. I just can't get enough of it, frankly.

C

1

a horoscope
b sometimes
c conversation
d doing

2

e university
f Internet

3

g used

4

h palms
i believed
j upside
k convinced
l future
m crystal balls

5

n stars

2

a 3
b 2
c 4
d 5
e 1

D

1

1 d
2 f
3 a
4 b
5 e
6 c
7 h
8 i
9 g

E

2

a 5
b 4
c 7
d 8
e 1
f 6
g 3
h 2

Speaking 3

C

1

One day Mary went shopping with her two children, Jake and Rachael. While they were getting some sweets, she went to buy a mop. Unfortunately a bucket fell off the shelves and hit her on the head. For a moment she was unconscious, and when she came to she couldn't remember who she was.
She walked out of the supermarket and straight into an army recruitment centre where she joined the army. Her husband and her children were left at home sad and unhappy.
A few weeks after she joined the army, she fell off a climbing frame and hit her head. Suddenly she remembered her husband and her children. She went to her commanding officer and explained the situation. He allowed her to leave the army, and she got home to her family.

Speaking 4

A

2

a Are you surprised?
b Was it a difficult exam? / Was the exam difficult?
c Would you like a biscuit?
d That's a nice car.
e It looks like it's going to rain.
f Shall we have / go for a drink?
g I'm starting a new job tomorrow.
h Phew! It's really hot.

3

Possible answers

a This could be anywhere. Perhaps someone has just made a surprising announcement, e.g. 'We're getting married', or 'I did really well in the exam!'
b This probably takes place in a student cafeteria, or in the student's house or home.
c This could be anywhere, but probably in A's house (B has come visiting).
d Outside on the street. Two people admiring B's car.
e Two people looking out of the window at a grey sky – or perhaps on a park or on the beach or out for a walk.
f Perhaps this is two people in the office at the end of the day, or two tourists who are feeling hot as they walk the streets.
g This sounds like a surprise announcement either in A's office or home, or out with friends.
h This conversation might be taking place on a beach, or perhaps it is two workers working hard.

B

1

a S – because of ellipsis.
b W – because of the full form of the auxiliary.
c W – or 'texting'.
d S – because we don't usually write this.
e S – *to be like* is only used in speaking.
f W – very formal full-form reported speech.
g W / S – could be either, but the use of the phrasal verb *put up with* suggests speaking.
h W – because of the verb *tolerate*.
i S
j S – but more formal than *i*.
k S – this kind of 'affirmative question' is used in speaking only.
l S
m S – the use of *check out* and the one-word exclamation *awesome* mean this must be spoken.
n W

C

1

a 4
b 7
c 3
d 6
e 10
f 1
g 11
h 9
i 12
j 2
k 8
l 5

2

a I / conv
b I / conv
c F / W
d F / W
e I / conv
f I / conv
g F / W
h F / W
i I / conv
j I / conv
k F / W
l I / conv

D

1

a S – it says S3 which means it's one of the top 3,000 words in speech, but it isn't a common word in writing, obviously.
b S – it says S2 which means it's one of the top 2,000 words in speech, but it isn't a common word in writing.
c W – it says W3 which means it's one of the top 3,000 words in written English, but it isn't a common word in speaking, obviously.
d W – it says W3 which means it's one of the top 3,000 words in written English, but it isn't a common word in speech.

E

1

All the *1* sentences are more informal and conversation-like.

All the *2* sentences are more formal and writing-like.

2

a be like / goes

b be like / goes

c goes

d be like

F

1

Examples of *a* are in blue (explanations are in brackets).

Examples of *b* are in red (explanations are in brackets).

Examples of *c* are in brown.

Oooh (to give an impression of wonder) you feel numb. The … you know it's a, it's a (to have time to think) saturation point. It's too much for you to digest that your grin is stuck on your face. It was stuck on my face for weeks. I would position that crown in such a way that as soon as I opened my eyes I would see my crown. I did that for weeks. It was such a great feeling. You just you're just (this is also an example of repetition as she is working out what to say) grinning and you are just numb. If that's what euphoria is, you know, umm (she's thinking as she speaks – *umm* gives her time to do this) you can't speak very clearly. You speak but you're just so excited you're tripping over your own words, and immediately there was a press conference on stage itself and it's like ooh ooh ooh (this gives a sense of wonder and excitement) because you go from being nobody, a regular person. That's not fair. It's not a nobody. You go from being a regular person to being in every newspaper around the world and everyone knows. It went from going in a bus with 87 other girls to 'and Miss World 1997 is Miss India' to a stretch limousine, bodyguards, where the heads of the company moved out of the presidential suite and I took over and chaperones and that's what it was right since then. You sit in the cockpits on take-offs and landings. You're treated like a queen you, you (she's thinking as she speaks) know, you have private planes, and all these flights and umm (she's thinking as she speaks) the red carpet and it's just lights! Camera! Action!